Home Office Research Study 230

Witness satisfaction: findings from the Witness Satisfaction Survey 2000

Emmy Whitehead

The views expressed in this report are those of the authors, not necessarily those of the Home Office (nor do they reflect Government policy).

Home Office Research, Development and Statistics Directorate
October 2001

Home Office Research Studies

The Home Office Research Studies are reports on research undertaken by or on behalf of the Home Office. They cover the range of subjects for which the Home Secretary has responsibility. Other publications produced by the Research, Development and Statistics Directorate include Findings, Statistical Bulletins and Statistical Papers.

The Research, Development and Statistics Directorate

RDS is part of the Home Office. The Home Office's purpose is to build a safe, just and tolerant society in which the rights and responsibilities of individuals, families and communities are properly balanced and the protection and security of the public are maintained.

RDS is also a part of the Government Statistical Service (GSS). One of the GSS aims is to inform Parliament and the citizen about the state of the nation and provide a window on the work and performance of government, allowing the impact of government policies and actions to be assessed.

Therefore -

Research Development and Statistics Directorate exists to improve policy making, decision taking and practice in support of the Home Office purpose and aims, to provide the public and Parliament with information necessary for informed debate and to publish information for future use.

First published 2001

Application for reproduction should be made to the Communications and Development Unit, Room 201, Home Office, 50 Queen Anne's Gate, London SW1H 9AT.

© Crown copyright 2001   ISBN 1 84082 735 1

ISSN 0072 6435

Foreword

The first national Witness Satisfaction Survey 2000 in England and Wales looks at levels of satisfaction of witnesses both generally and specifically with their treatment by the different key agencies within the criminal justice system. It covers prosecution and defence witnesses in both the Crown Court and magistrates' courts. It shows that 76 per cent of witnesses were satisfied with their overall experience, but that satisfaction was generally higher for individual agencies.

Levels of satisfaction were strongly related to the verdict, the amount of information given to witnesses, feelings of intimidation, facilities at court, waiting times and convenience of court date. Despite the relatively high level of satisfaction with their overall experience, only 61 per cent of witnesses said they would be happy to be a witness again.

All agencies have a role to play in helping to increase witness satisfaction, both with the individual agency involved, but also overall. The experience of giving evidence can probably never be made pleasant, but a range of relatively straightforward amendments to the way in which witnesses are dealt with may go a long way towards removing some of the main concerns.

David Moxon
Head of Crime and Criminal Justice Unit
Research Development and Statistics Directorate

Acknowledgements

I would like to thank Robin Elliott and David Brown for their continued help and support throughout the writing of this publication. I would also like to thank Robert Street for his involvement in the earlier stages of the project and for all the advice he gave me. Thanks also go to court staff and the Witness Service who helped in the recruitment stage, as well as to BMRB interviewers, and to Sally Malam and Helen Angle from BMRB who were involved in all stages of questionnaire design, recruitment and fieldwork. A large thank you also goes to all respondents who agreed to be interviewed.

Emmy Whitehead

Contents

List of tables

List of figures

Appendix tables

Summary

Introduction

Over recent years there has been an increasing interest in monitoring and improving the standards of service provided to members of the public by government and the public services. The criminal justice system has been no exception and high level aims and objectives have been set. Thus, the CJS Strategic Plan 1999–2002 contains the objective: "to meet the needs of victims, witnesses and jurors within the system". This supports the broader aim "to dispense justice fairly and efficiently and to promote confidence in the rule of law". The agencies of the criminal justice system have a joint performance target to improve, by five percentage points, the satisfaction level of witnesses with their treatment by the system by 2002, and thereafter at least maintain that level of performance.

Hitherto, witnesses' experiences of the criminal justice system had been subject only to limited monitoring. A special survey, carried out on a national basis, was therefore devised to gauge witnesses' perceptions in a comprehensive manner. The main aim was to obtain a broad indication of the level of satisfaction of witnesses both generally and specifically with their treatment by the different key agencies within the criminal justice system. For the purposes of the survey, these agencies were: the police; the CPS/prosecution lawyers; defence lawyers; court staff; judges and magistrates; Victim Support; and the Witness Service.

Methods

Witnesses were recruited at all Crown Court centres and about 40 per cent of magistrates' courts in late May and early June 2000. Witnesses were approached directly at court and asked to take part in the survey. Those who agreed were then interviewed at a later date (after the verdict in the case was given) and away from the court.

The survey covered both prosecution and defence witnesses. Expert witnesses, police witnesses and others giving evidence in a professional capacity were excluded from the survey. Almost 2,500 witnesses were interviewed.

Main findings

- About three-quarters (76%) of witnesses said they were very or fairly satisfied with their overall experience of the criminal justice system.

- Satisfaction with individual agencies was generally higher, and especially high for the Witness Service (97%), court staff (96%) and judges and magistrates (95%).

- However, the fact that nearly a quarter of witnesses were dissatisfied overall suggests that there is scope for improvement within the system.

- Levels of overall satisfaction were strongly related to the verdict, amount of information given to witnesses, feelings of intimidation (both personal and by the process), facilities at court, and waiting times and convenience of date.

- Overall satisfaction varied considerably between victims and other witnesses. Thus, 67 per cent of victims were satisfied compared with 80 per cent of other prosecution witnesses and 77 per cent of defence witnesses.

- Age, sex and court type (i.e. magistrates' or Crown) were not strongly linked with satisfaction.

- Although 76 per cent of witnesses said they were satisfied with their experience at court, only 61 per cent of witnesses said they would be happy to be a witness again.

- Satisfaction with the experience of being a witness did not necessarily point to willingness to be a witness again; a fifth of those who were satisfied would not want to be a witness again. Only 6 per cent of dissatisfied witnesses would be happy to be a witness again.

- Willingness to be a witness again was strongly linked with intimidation, verdict, convenience of court date and satisfaction with facilities at court, with those who were dissatisfied in relation to these aspects being less keen to give evidence in any future trial.

Conclusions and recommendations

Satisfaction with individual agencies' performance is generally high (around the 90% mark). However, overall satisfaction with the experience of being a witness is at a somewhat lower level (76%). There are a number of reasons which might help explain this difference. Dissatisfaction relating to the four key areas identified above (intimidation, information, facilities and waiting times) does not necessarily fall entirely on one agency. Also, witnesses might be generally satisfied with the performance of each agency, but still have feelings of dissatisfaction overall because the experience of giving evidence at court may never be pleasant.

Each agency has a role to play in helping increase witness satisfaction, both with the individual agency involved, but also overall. Focusing on practical measures to increase information, reduce intimidation, improve facilities at court, and reduce waiting times would go a long way towards addressing the concerns which witnesses expressed during the survey and perhaps help to raise overall satisfaction even beyond the fairly high level at which it is currently pitched. While verdict and convenience of court date are also important, these are more difficult areas to address.

Information:
- Each agency has a responsibility for this, and appropriate information must be made available by each individual agency and at every stage – both before witnesses arrive at court, and during the day while they wait to give evidence.

- Early notification of court dates might help reduce the numbers of witnesses finding the dates very inconvenient.

Intimidation:
- Each agency can be involved at different stages in helping identify witness intimidation, in reassuring witnesses and in providing the support they require.

- In cases which involve vulnerable and intimidated witnesses, all possible help should be provided to reduce intimidation. Once the special measures designed to help vulnerable and intimidated witnesses give best evidence (contained in the Youth Justice and Criminal Evidence Act 1999) come into force, the scope for this will substantially increase.

Court facilities:

- Familiarisation visits to court can help witnesses know what facilities are available to them.

- Showing witnesses the court facilities on arrival may help make witnesses feel more at ease.

Waiting times:

- When the court knows there is going to be a delay, non-victim witnesses could be given the opportunity to leave the courtroom and be called back nearer the time they are needed to give evidence.

- Before witnesses arrive at court they should be informed about possible waiting times.

Future sweeps of the survey will monitor the performance of the criminal justice system against these measures, as well as in increasing witness satisfaction overall and with individual agencies.

1.   Introduction

Background to the research

There has been a growing concentration on the needs of victims (many of whom are witnesses) over recent years. This interest was fuelled by early British Crime Surveys (BCS) in the 1980s, which provided detailed information for the first time about the victim's perspective and levels of victimisation in England and Wales. Government policies aimed at giving victims a more central, less marginalised place in the Criminal Justice System (CJS) have drawn on the increasing awareness of victim's issues generated by the BCS, and also by the creation of Victim Support.[1]

The first Victim's Charter was published in 1990. It described how the CJS worked and gave examples of good practice in the treatment of victims of crime. The Charter was a major step in seeking to ensure that victims started to receive better treatment from the CJS. The Victim's Charter was revised in 1996, and for the first time there was a statement of the standards of service victims of crime can expect.[2]

Many victims are also witnesses, who play a vital role in ensuring that offenders are brought to justice. Concerns about the treatment of witnesses are therefore a natural offshoot of concern with victims. However, some of the concerns are specific to being a witness. It should be recognised that not all witnesses are victims. Some are bystanders who witness crime happening to others; and others are witnesses for the defence. (The creation of a Witness Service (WS) in the Crown Court, now being extended to magistrates' courts, reflects this awareness.) Central concerns are those connected with intimidation and the ordeal of giving evidence in court. Home Office research (Maynard, 1994) on witness intimidation, the creation of new offences of witness intimidation and the government report (Speaking up for Justice, 1998) on vulnerable and intimidated witnesses reflected these concerns. Another theme has been the treatment of witnesses who are called to give evidence at court. A dedicated sub-group of the Trial Issues Group deals with issues relating to witness care.[3] Among the aspects of witness treatment which are routinely monitored are witness waiting times and the proportion of witnesses who were not required to give evidence.

---

1   A National Association of Victims Support Schemes (NAVASS) was created in 1980, and was the precursor to Victim Support.

2   A review of the Victim's Charter was underway at the time of writing: see www.homeoffice.gov.uk/cpd/pvu/vcreviewindex.htm for further details.

3   The Trial Issues Group (otherwise known as TIG) was a national level inter-agency group, involving representatives from across the criminal justice system, in planning and co-ordinating measures to dispense justice fairly and efficiently. See www.cjsonline.org/legal/cjcc_tig.htm for further details. TIG has now been replaced with a different group chaired by John Gieve, Permanent Secretary.

The trend in recent years to set measurable aims and objectives for government has included witnesses within its ambit. The CJS Strategic Plan 1999–2002 contains the objective: "to meet the needs of victims, witnesses and jurors within the system". This supports the broader aim "to dispense justice fairly and efficiently and to promote confidence in the rule of law". The plan identifies performance measures and targets so that the outcome of work supporting this objective can be assessed. The relevant measure in relation to witnesses is their level of satisfaction with their treatment in the CJS. In the absence of data which directly measured satisfaction levels, a survey was commissioned in early 2000 in order to provide baseline information. The survey was developed and managed by the Home Office's Research Development and Statistics Directorate with the agreement and support of the Lord Chancellor's Department and the Court Service, as well as the inter-agency Trials Issues Group's Witness Care Sub-Group (which dealt with witness issues at the time of the research).[4] It also had the agreement of the Senior Presiding Judge for England and Wales.

The aims of the research

The main aim was to obtain a broad indication of the level of satisfaction of witnesses generally and with their treatment by the different key agencies within the CJS. For the purposes of the survey these were defined as: the police; the CPS/prosecution lawyers; defence lawyers; court staff; judges and magistrates; Victim Support (VS); and the Witness Service (WS). A witness was defined as 'someone who is involved in a case listed for trial and who has been asked to attend court as a witness'. Future sweeps of the survey will be able to measure whether the levels of witness satisfaction show any change over time in response to the various initiatives aimed at improving services to witnesses. The first Witness Satisfaction Survey (WSS) was conducted for the Home Office by an independent organisation, BMRB.

Methodology

Recruitment of the sample

Two alternative methods of recruiting witnesses for the survey were initially considered. One was to recruit witnesses to take part in the survey at court, approaching them either before or just after giving evidence. The other possibility was to send out a written invitation to all those whom police records showed had been called to give evidence in a criminal trial. The first method was chosen as it was felt that it would lead to the recruitment of a more

---

4   The WCSG has now been discontinued. The structure and responsibilities of its replacement were still being discussed at the time of writing.

representative sample. If participation depended on response to a letter it was felt that the sample might be skewed towards particular segments of the witness population: for example, those who were most dissatisfied. Requiring positive action from witnesses might also result in a low response rate. There were also difficulties in relation to data protection and the workload involved for the police with the second method and fears that witnesses with anti-police views might not respond well to an approach via the police. In addition this method of approach would not capture defence witnesses.

Witnesses were recruited at all Crown Court centres and 159 out of about 430 magistrates' courts[5] in late May and early June 2000. Witnesses were approached directly at court and asked to take part in the survey. Victim Support (VS)[6] agreed to their Witness Service (WS)[7] co-ordinators and volunteers carrying out the task of approaching witnesses in the courts where this service operates. It was also agreed that court staff and ushers would assist with the recruitment process.[8] This was especially important in courts where the Witness Service was not operating. Those witnesses who agreed to take part were asked to provide contact details and were then interviewed at a later date (after the verdict in the case was given) and away from the court.

The survey covered both prosecution and defence witnesses, whether or not required to give evidence when they attended court. Expert witnesses, police witnesses and others giving evidence in a professional capacity (e.g. Customs and Excise officers, Department of Social Security officers) were excluded from the survey. Child witnesses (witnesses aged under 17) were also included in the survey, but were only interviewed with parental or guardian consent.

The sampling frame for the survey was based upon estimates of the number of witnesses attending court derived from the Joint Performance Management Witness Attendance at Court monitoring scheme run by the Lord Chancellor's Department (LCD) on behalf of the Trials Issues Group.[9]

---

5   The number of magistrates' courts in England and Wales was 428 in January 2001.
6   Victim Support (VS) is an independent charity receiving government financial support. VS volunteers offer emotional and financial support to victims of crime and their families once a crime has taken place, as well as providing information about other organisations which may be able to help with specific problems. Before a case comes to court, contact with Victim Support is usually arranged though the police.
7   The Witness Service (WS) is run by Victim Support. Trained volunteers supported by Witness Service staff deliver the service. At present, the Witness Service is based in all Crown Court centres in England and Wales and some magistrates' courts. It provides information and support to witnesses. It is planned to extend the coverage of the Witness Service to all magistrates' courts by April 2002.
8   This was agreed with the Lord Chancellor's Department for magistrates' courts and Court Service regarding the Crown Court.
9   Based on results of June 1998 Joint Performance Management witness monitoring survey and Court Service statistics. These gave the estimated total number of witnesses at the Crown Court and at magistrates' courts.

Of witnesses approached at the recruitment stage, 61 per cent agreed to participate. Interviews were achieved with 73 per cent of the eligible sample, giving a total final sample of nearly 2,500. Telephone interviews were conducted with 78 per cent of respondents and face-to-face interviews with the remainder. The face-to-face sample included all witnesses aged 17 or under, witnesses to sexual offences, witnesses with learning difficulties and those who had problems with English.

Interviews were conducted with 2498 people: 29 per cent were victims, 58 per cent other prosecution witnesses and 13 per cent defence witnesses. Child witnesses formed 7 per cent of the sample. Fifty-six per cent were male, 44 per cent female. Crown Court witnesses made up 44 per cent of the sample, magistrates' court witnesses 56 per cent.

The survey asked witnesses in detail about all aspects of their experience as a witness, from first contact with the police through to giving evidence and beyond.[10]

In all courts in selected regions with high ethnic minority populations a booster sample of witnesses from ethnic minorities was approached for recruitment. It was hoped that an extra 500 interviews would thereby be achieved. In fact, only just over 100 were achieved. There was a higher refusal rate than there was in the recruitment for the main sample. Possible reasons for the higher refusal rate include:

- Court staff may have been less willing to approach only witnesses from ethnic minorities;

- the extended recruitment period of five weeks for the ethnic boost may have resulted in 'survey fatigue' as those tasked with recruiting witnesses forgot or became increasingly reluctant to approach witnesses; and

- ethnic minority witnesses may have been less inclined to take part in the survey due to greater suspicion of its purposes and possible language difficulties.

With the ethnic boost included, 11 per cent of interviews were with ethnic minority witnesses; without it, it would have been 7 per cent. The number of ethnic minority witnesses interviewed was not enough to draw any firm conclusions about differences in the satisfaction or experiences of ethnic minorities. Consideration will be given to improving the ethnic boost in the next sweep of the survey.

---

10 Copies of the Witness Satisfaction Survey 2000 questionnaire are available upon request.

Other recruitment issues

The Witness Service has contact with fewer defence witnesses than prosecution witnesses, which made recruiting these witnesses harder. It was estimated from the LCD Witness Monitoring Exercise that of witnesses approached, 21 per cent would be expected to be defence witnesses. The proportion of defence witnesses in the Witness Satisfaction Survey was 13 per cent.

Interviews were only conducted with witnesses once the verdict had been reached. Finding out when verdicts were reached in cases proved to be problematic at times. In a large number of cases, verdict dates were unknown, and not all completed cases could be identified.

The survey did not include witnesses who fail to turn up at court. Attempts to devise a workable methodology for identifying and contacting such witnesses were not successful. It is also highly likely that, had members of this group been contacted, they would have been reluctant to respond for fear of official sanctions being taken against them for their non-attendance.

Weighting was applied to the data to compensate for deliberate under-sampling of smaller magistrates' courts and over-sampling of some of the larger Crown Courts.

Satisfaction research

There are a number of other surveys and studies on satisfaction with the CJS, although none directed specifically at witnesses. The British Crime Survey (BCS) measures crimes against people living in private households in England and Wales. It also covers a variety of other crime-related issues, including attitudes to the police and attitudes towards sentencing. The BCS is better at measuring victim satisfaction and victim intimidation than the experiences of witnesses. This is because relatively few witnesses to crime are ever required to give evidence at court and, therefore, their experience of the CJS remains relatively limited. However, comparable questions between the BCS and the Witness Satisfaction Survey include ones relating to confidence in the criminal justice system, and satisfaction with the police and Victim Support.[11]

The Lord Chancellor's Department (LCD) have carried out or commissioned a number of satisfaction surveys relating to various aspects of the court system including juror satisfaction, magistrates' court waiting times for defendants, and the views of magistrates' courts users on facilities and information provided at court. There is also the *Joint*

---

11 Wherever possible, to maximise comparability, question wording in the WSS was consistent with the BCS.

Performance Management Witness Monitoring Survey which looks at how many witnesses are called, how many attend and how long they wait before being called to give evidence. Finally, the *User Satisfaction Survey*, commissioned by the Court Service, covers members of the public who had used the civil courts, professionals at both the civil and criminal courts, and jurors.

There are also some smaller-scale studies which are relevant. For example, Plotnikoff and Woolfson (1997) interviewed witnesses attending magistrates' courts including the youth court in order to record their experiences of being a witness and their views on the kind of support they required. They also interviewed key figures in government departments, those involved with the running of magistrates' courts and Victim Support. The research aims included looking at the treatment of witnesses and the improvement of witness care.

Southgate and Grosvenor (2000) also carried out a small-scale qualitative survey to explore the kinds of things that are related to confidence in the CJS, which covered different users of the CJS.

The work described above has covered some of the areas of interest in relation to witnesses: for instance satisfaction at court and levels of confidence. However, these other surveys do not focus solely on witnesses, and it was therefore felt necessary to carry out a larger scale quantitative survey covering all aspects of being a witness in court and experiences of the CJS.

Structure of the report

Chapter 2 focuses on the period leading up to arrival at court, from first contact with the police. It addresses issues such as satisfaction with the police, concerns and worries about being a witness, the amount of information received prior to arrival at court, and convenience of trial date. Chapter 3 looks first at what happens at court before witnesses give evidence, and then moves on to examine the process of giving evidence in the courtroom. Finally the chapter looks at what happens after giving evidence: for instance, whether witnesses are happy with the verdict, whether they feel intimidated (although intimidation could be experienced before giving evidence as well) and whether they have any suggestions for improvements. Chapter 4 identifies how happy witnesses would be to act as a witness again, and how this relates to overall satisfaction and satisfaction with individual agencies. The results of multivariate analysis are presented, showing which factors are most strongly associated with satisfaction. Chapter 5 draws out some conclusions and considers the policy implications of these findings.

2.   Witnesses' experiences pre-trial

This chapter looks first at the role of the police in relation to witnesses. It examines: how many (and which) witnesses had contact with the police; whether the police kept witnesses informed; witnesses' perceptions of how courteously they were dealt with; and whether they were satisfied with the treatment they received. The chapter then considers any worries or concerns witnesses may have had before coming to court. It discusses contact with Victim Support (VS) and draws comparisons with British Crime Survey (BCS) findings. Finally, the chapter considers the provision of information to witnesses about what being a witness involves.

Contact with the police

For most witnesses of crime, the first contact they have with officialdom is with the police and their initial impressions are undoubtedly important in shaping satisfaction with the CJS as a whole. Among all witnesses, 86 per cent recalled having contact with the police. Prosecution witnesses were more likely to have had contact (91%), compared with defence witnesses (52%). This is probably because defence witnesses were more likely to have been approached by the defendant's lawyer, rather than by the police. It could also be related to use of character witnesses by the defence.

Among witnesses who had contact with the police, 47 per cent volunteered information to the police (63% of victims, 40% of other prosecution and 32% of defence witnesses), the remainder being asked by the police for help.

Satisfaction with the police

Among witnesses who had contact with the police, 58 per cent were very satisfied and 31 per cent were fairly satisfied with the way they were treated (88% in total). There are no directly comparable questions in the British Crime Survey. However, the BCS 2000 found that 78 per cent of those surveyed thought that their local police did a very or fairly good job (Sims and Myhill, 2000). The BCS did ask victims whether they were satisfied with the way the police dealt with the matter: 58 per cent were satisfied. However, unlike victim witnesses in the present survey, relatively few of the victims surveyed in the BCS had an offender brought to justice and this may explain the lower level of satisfaction reported. The

Witness Satisfaction Survey found that 86 per cent of victim witnesses were satisfied with the way they were treated by the police (compared with 91% of other prosecution and 78% of defence witnesses).

The single most important factor related to satisfaction with the police was whether witnesses felt the police treated them courteously. Over 90 per cent of all witnesses felt that they were treated courteously by the police (94% of prosecution and 87% of defence witnesses). Among witnesses who felt that the police treated them courteously, 92 per cent were satisfied,[12] whereas only 30 per cent were satisfied when they were not treated courteously. However, among victims who felt that they were not treated courteously, almost 50 per cent were still satisfied with the police. Other factors (particularly whether they provided enough information – see below) were also important in determining satisfaction. Again, it seems likely that for prosecution witnesses ultimately the most important issue is whether the offender is identified and a case brought to court.[13]

Defence witnesses were less satisfied with their treatment by the police (78% were satisfied) compared with prosecution witnesses (89% were satisfied) (Table A.1 in Appendix). However, looking just at witnesses who gave a statement to the police, satisfaction increased among all witnesses, but especially defence witnesses, to 86 per cent. It is not clear whether this is because defence witnesses tend to see the police as being on the side of the prosecution, or whether it is because there are differences in how they are treated.

Male witnesses and child witnesses (witnesses aged under 17) were more likely to be satisfied than females and young adults. Children, perhaps, tend to be less critical and more accepting of how they are treated. The police may also be especially good at dealing with child witnesses. It is less easy to explain the differences between males and females. This may reflect a real difference in treatment but it is equally possible that it reflects different expectations among males and females.

Intimidation

Witnesses were asked whether there was any point in the whole process when they felt intimidated, either by an individual or by the whole process or the court environment. Witnesses who felt intimidated were also less satisfied with the police. Among those who felt

---

12 Unless otherwise indicated 'satisfied' means very or fairly satisfied.
13 Although the decision to prosecute rests with the CPS, the police role in putting cases together which are strong enough to lead to a prosecution is obviously crucial.

intimidated by both an individual and by the process as a whole, 72 per cent were satisfied, compared with 92 per cent of witnesses who reported no feelings of intimidation. Dissatisfaction with the police among those who experienced intimidation may have arisen because they thought that the police should have done something but felt that they had not. Intimidation is discussed further in Chapter 3.

Being kept informed

When the police took statements from witnesses, the majority recalled being informed that they might be called to give evidence at court – 90 per cent of prosecution and 83 per cent of defence witnesses. Satisfaction with the police was higher among witnesses who recalled being told that they might be called as a witness (90%), than among those who did not recall being told anything (77%).

Table 2.1: *How regularly witnesses were kept informed about the progress of the case, by witness type (percentages)*

	Regularly kept informed	Occasionally kept informed	Not kept informed at all
Prosecution			
Victim	26	30	44
Other	16	24	61
All	19	26	55
Defence	16	16	68
Total	19	25	56

Base: All who gave a statement to the police. Unweighted N=2079.
Note: Excludes 'don't knows'.

Despite the great majority of witnesses being told that they might be required to give evidence, only a minority said that they were then kept regularly informed about the progress of the case. Victims were more likely to say they were kept regularly informed by the police (26%) than non-victims (16%). This may reflect the increasing concern in recent years to pay attention to the needs of the victim, as well as the pragmatic consideration that the victim is integral to the case. Police officers may also assume that victims are more interested in the case than other witnesses. Victims may have more concerns about the case and about going to court than other witnesses, and the police can play a role in informing them about any changes to the case and what is likely to happen at court. However, 44 per cent of victims and over half of all witnesses said that they were not kept informed at all about the progress of the case (Table 2.1). Under the Victim's Charter (Home Office, 1996) there is a standard that the police should keep victims informed of significant developments[14] in the case.

The survey did not ask witnesses how much information they would have liked on case progress, but it would seem that keeping witnesses informed was associated both with satisfaction with the police and overall satisfaction. Thus, among witnesses who were kept regularly informed, satisfaction with the police reached 98 per cent, whereas when witnesses were not kept informed at all, satisfaction with the police was lower (at 83%). This pattern was similar for both prosecution and defence witnesses. Witnesses' overall satisfaction with the way they were treated by the criminal justice system was strongly linked with how well they were kept informed by the police: 83 per cent of those who said they were kept regularly informed were satisfied, compared with 71 per cent of those who said they were not kept informed at all.

Contact with Victim Support

Victim Support volunteers are available to offer information, help and support to victims of crime and their families, once a crime has taken place. Contact with Victim Support is usually arranged through the police before a case comes to court. Under the Victim's Charter (Home Office, 1996) details of victims of burglary, assault, robbery, theft (except from and of cars), arson, harassment or damage to the victim's home, are usually passed automatically by the police to Victim Support. In cases involving sexual offences, domestic violence and homicide, details will only be given to Victim Support if the victim agrees[15].

In the Witness Satisfaction Survey (WSS), 35 per cent of victim witnesses had contact with Victim Support. This was higher among victims of a violent or sexual offence (42%) than victims of other offences (26%). The 1998 BCS also found that victims of violence were more likely to be in contact with Victim Support. The British Crime Survey covers in detail victims' experiences of and public perceptions of Victim Support (see Maguire and Kynch, 2000). The BCS covers all victims, whether or not they report crimes and whether or not those who report are ever required to give evidence at court. The WSS, however, only covers those witnesses who are called to give evidence at court. According to the BCS, 58

---

14 Significant developments are defined as 1) arrest and charge/caution 2) any substantial alterations to charge 3) date of court hearing and 4) case outcome.

15 Victim Support's code of practice reiterates the above, but omits 'harassment' from its list of offences to be referred automatically.

per cent of victims found Victim Support very or fairly helpful. The WSS found that the majority of witnesses who had contact with Victim Support were very or fairly satisfied with their treatment (88%). This higher proportion feeling satisfied might be due to victim witnesses being more likely to feel well disposed towards Victim Support because an offender has been caught.

Concerns about attending court

Over half of witnesses expressed concern about being a witness at court. Victims were more likely than non-victims to have been worried. There are a number of reasons why this might be the case, including greater anxieties about seeing the defendant, and concerns about possible repercussions from either the defendant or the defendant's family. Victims may also feel on trial themselves, or experience feelings of guilt or blame for what happened. Despite the existence of court powers to restrict media reporting, Lees (1996) found victims of sexual offences were frightened because they felt they were on trial rather than the defendant. The Youth Justice and Criminal Evidence Act 1999 has now placed these powers to restrict media reporting on a statutory footing, as well as introducing a range of special measures which are designed to reduce the stress in giving evidence for vulnerable and intimidated witnesses[16].

Table 2.2 shows that females and children were the most likely to have expressed some level of overall concern about giving evidence (68% and 69% respectively). For a minority of adults (22%) previous experience of giving evidence may help reduce the stress of the experience because they know what to expect, but this was true for hardly any child witnesses (only 2%). The majority of children were prosecution witnesses (96%) and just over half (51%) were victims (compared with 27% of adults). The concerns noted above, for example about victims feeling they are on trial, are therefore particularly relevant for child witnesses. Some special measures are currently available to assist child witnesses to give best evidence (a separate survey of vulnerable witnesses is examining these in detail). They include: video-taped evidence; provision of pagers; being escorted to and from the court; and special communication methods in the courtroom – for instance giving evidence via a video link. The Witness Satisfaction Survey found that 14 per cent of child witnesses gave evidence to the police that was video-taped. Just over a quarter (28%) of child witnesses were provided with a volunteer (for example from Victim Support or the Police Family Protection Unit) to accompany them to court.

---

16 The majority of these measures are awaiting implementation and it is therefore too early to say what impact they have had on court practice.

Witnesses were more likely to feel worried overall when the defendant was charged with either a sexual or violent offence (61% compared with 50% for other offences). These findings are not surprising in the light of the conclusions of the literature review contained in *Speaking up for Justice*. These stated that there was a lack of confidence among victims of sexual offences in the ability of the criminal justice system to convict the perpetrator. The report also mentioned the fact that the trial is often seen among victims as being as bad an experience as the original offence. Worries about going to court in sexual offence cases are also likely to be higher because cross-examination tends to be more severe. Whatever the offence, female witnesses were more likely to have expressed concerns about appearing at court (68%) than male witnesses (46%) (Table A.2 in Appendix).

Table 2.2: Percentage of witnesses feeling worried

		Worried overall	General worries	Meeting or seeing the defendant
Witness type				
	Victim	63	17	23
	Other prosecution	54	15	14
	Defence	45	18	4
Sex				
	Male	46	11	12
	Female	68	24	20
Court type				
	Crown	60	19	16
	Magistrates'	52	14	15
Age				
	Under 17	69	21	35
	17–34	59	17	16
	35–54	53	15	13
	55+	49	16	9
Ethnicity				
	White	56	17	15
	Black	56	17	21
	Asian	43	7	13
	Other	63	12	23
Total		56	16	15

Base: All witnesses. Unweighted N=2498.
Notes: 1. Excludes 'don't knows'.
2. 'Worried overall' relates to all witnesses who expressed concern.

Almost two-thirds (64%) of witnesses who said that they had a long standing illness, disability or infirmity felt worried, compared with 54 per cent of those who did not. Witnesses were also asked whether or not they needed any help in getting to court. Among witnesses who felt that they needed such help (for example, those with mobility problems or transport problems), 71 per cent felt concerned about being a witness, compared with 55 per cent of other witnesses.

Knowledge about the court system appeared to be an important factor associated with levels of concern prior to coming to court. Those who had been a witness before and those who felt familiar with court procedures were less likely to feel worried about coming to court. For instance, 47 per cent of witnesses who said they were familiar with court procedures expressed concern, compared with 62 per cent of those who said they were not familiar.

Witnesses were asked whether there was anything in particular about being a witness that they were worried or concerned about. The most common concerns were general worries or pre-court nerves, and worries about meeting or seeing the defendant. Seventeen per cent of victims were worried about the former and almost a quarter (23%) of victims were worried about the latter. Children were particularly likely to express concern about meeting the defendant. Witnesses at the Crown Court were more likely to suffer from pre-court nerves than magistrates' courts witnesses. This is probably because more serious cases are heard at the Crown Court, and also due to the formality of the Crown Court setting.

Other concerns included: repercussions/harassment during the case (6%); repercussions after the case (5%); being cross-examined/the defendant's legal team (4%); having never been a witness before (4%); and poor communication with the court (3%).

Information about attending court

It is important that witnesses are prepared for the task of giving evidence by being given information about going to court and what is expected of them there. The amount of information witnesses received varied substantially. Nearly 80 per cent of prosecution witnesses and 72 per cent of defence witnesses recalled receiving some information about being a witness before they went to court. Almost a quarter (23%) of prosecution witnesses, and 10 per cent of defence witnesses recalled being given this information by the police. Over a third of children (34%) were kept informed by the police. Almost three-quarters (74%) of witnesses recalled receiving information through either the 'Witness in Court' leaflet or another leaflet. About one third of children (34%) remembered receiving a child witness information pack,[17] and 31 per cent of children recalled having contact with a child witness or liaison officer or some other individual who could answer questions about being a child witness.

Defence witnesses were significantly less likely than prosecution witnesses to have remembered receiving a letter informing them that they would be called as a witness (57% compared with 91%). Defence witnesses should be told when to attend by the defendants' solicitor rather than by the police. A quarter of defence witnesses received information about being a witness from their lawyers. It is possible that some others were told by the police.

Table 2.3: **Whether witnesses received adequate information about being a witness at court (percentages)**

	Enough information	Some information but need more	No information
Time involved in being a witness	29	11	59
What needed to bring	28	4	69
Time needed to arrive	88	8	4
Directions to court	61	5	34
What to do on arrival	51	8	41
What would happen in court	52	12	36

Base: All witnesses. Unweighted N=2498.
Note: Excludes 'don't knows'.

The type of information provided and its adequacy also varied substantially (Table 2.3). Witnesses claimed that they were least informed about the time involved in being a witness (59% said they received no information), and what they needed to bring to court (69% said they received no information), for instance something to read whilst waiting.

Figure 2.1 shows that witnesses' overall satisfaction with their experience at court was closely related to how well they were kept informed.

---

17 Now called a family information pack.

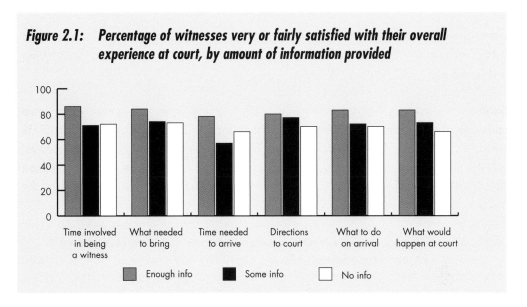

Figure 2.1: *Percentage of witnesses very or fairly satisfied with their overall experience at court, by amount of information provided*

Witnesses who were given enough information about the different aspects of being a witness at court were more likely to feel satisfied with the overall experience than those who were given no information at all.

Defence witnesses were less likely to feel they had been given enough information about being a witness at court (Table A2.3 in Appendix). For example, over two-thirds of defence witnesses (71%) were not informed (and did not know) that they could be accompanied to court by a friend or relative, compared with 49 per cent of non-victim prosecution witnesses and 33 per cent of victims. It should be noted that contact with defence witnesses would predominantly be by defence solicitors and not the police. A higher proportion of female witnesses were informed (or knew) that they could be accompanied (58%) compared with male witnesses (49%). Child witnesses were the most likely to be informed or have known (89%). This kind of information is very simple to impart to witnesses and is of obvious value. It may be that practitioners take for granted that witnesses already have this kind of basic knowledge and are more likely to mention it to those witnesses they perceive as needing additional support.

When witnesses were informed that they would be called as a witness at court, the majority were given an actual date of the case (70%), with the other 30 per cent being given a rough idea of when the trial would be, followed up later by the actual date. A third of witnesses were told the date of the court case over a month in advance, and a further 47 per cent were told one week to a month before. Seven percent of witnesses, however, were only told the day or evening before they were expected at court. The majority of these (6%), were Crown Court witnesses. The short notice given to the witnesses could be considered not unusual since cases at the Crown Court can fold at the last minute due to guilty pleas being entered. Also, these courts tend to engage in involved legal arguments which are difficult to forecast as to their duration. Trials at the Crown Court can go on for weeks, and so if a trial suddenly collapses, the vacated space is quickly given to another trial. This helps to explain the short notice sometimes given to witnesses.

Convenience of court date

While less than half (45%) of defence witnesses recalled being asked whether there were any dates when they would be unable to attend court, more than three-quarters (76%) of prosecution witnesses recalled being asked. Crown Court witnesses were more likely to say that they had been asked (79%, compared with 66% of magistrates' court witnesses). This may be due to the fact that cases at the Crown Court tend to last longer and may be hard to re-schedule, thereby creating the need for dates to be checked with witnesses. The courts list cases, and it is the responsibility of the police, prosecution and defence solicitors for obtaining and providing the court with witnesses' availability. Over 70 per cent of adult witnesses said they were asked about dates when they would be unable to attend. However, child witnesses (or their parents/guardians) only recalled being asked in 51 per cent of cases. It is not clear whether this simply reflects a difference in recall or a genuine difference in consultation. If the latter, it may have been assumed that child witnesses are more likely to be able to attend court at any given date than adults, who are likely to have other responsibilities, such as work. However, the child's parents or guardians would still need to be consulted, so this is not a complete explanation.

When asked how convenient it was to attend court on the date given, 56 per cent said it was convenient, 29 per cent slightly inconvenient and 16 per cent very inconvenient. There was a significant difference between older and younger witnesses, with 73 per cent of witnesses aged 55+ saying it was convenient, compared with 51 per cent of 17–34 year olds. This undoubtedly reflects age differences in lifestyles and employment status.

Overall satisfaction with treatment by the CJS was associated with convenience of the court date. Among witnesses who found the date convenient, 82 per cent were satisfied with their overall experience, compared with only 57 per cent of those who found it very inconvenient.

Changes to the court date

Thirty-nine per cent of witnesses said that the original date of the court case was changed; 44 per cent of these changes were made on the day set for witnesses' attendance. Among the 56 per cent of witnesses who were informed of the change before the day just over one-fifth were only told the day before. Changes to court dates were more likely to be made before the day set for witnesses' attendance at the Crown Court (66%) than at magistrates' courts (42%). Cases at the Crown Court, which are more likely to overrun, tend to be longer, which should make it easier to inform witnesses of any delays to their case before the day. At magistrates' courts there are more cases scheduled in one day and there is less chance of knowing before the day whether a case is not going to be heard. The central problem for the courts is that of balancing efficiency in use of court time with convenience for witnesses.

Whether the date for witnesses' attendance was changed was associated with their overall satisfaction with their treatment by the criminal justice system. Thus, where the trial date was not changed, 80 per cent of witnesses were satisfied, compared with 70 per cent when there was a change to the date. However, satisfaction was more strongly associated with the timing of the information about the change in date. Eighty-six per cent of witnesses who were informed over a month before were satisfied, compared with 60 per cent who were told the day before. Clearly, witnesses who are given ample warning of a date change have more time to prepare – whether in terms of agreeing time off with an employer or simply readying themselves psychologically for the ordeal of giving evidence. Changing dates could make witnesses more upset or anxious about going to court, especially when they were only told the day before or on the day itself. Having mentally prepared themselves once for the task, they now faced the prospect of having to go through the same stressful build-up a second time.

Pre-court visits

The Witness Service[18] is responsible for organising pre-court visits. On resource grounds, this facility cannot be offered to all witnesses and the Service therefore focuses on those witnesses who they think will benefit most from such a visit. A pre-court visit enables witnesses to see the layout of the court and where they will be situated when they give evidence. This may help to make the experience on the day a little less daunting.

---

18 Chapter 3 contains more details about the role of the Witness Service.

The survey found that one in ten witnesses had a visit to court before the day of the trial. Of those who did not, only around a quarter were aware that a pre-court visit could be organised. The survey suggests most witnesses are anxious about attending court. Having a visit prior to their court case may help relieve some of the pressures on the day. The survey, however, showed that witnesses who had a pre-court visit were more likely to have said they were concerned about being a witness (64%) than those who had not (55%). This may suggest that visits are generally well targeted at those who have most need of them rather than the visit itself actually adds to the anxiety. Many of those who did not have a visit may not have felt in need of one.

Crown Court witnesses were more likely to have had a pre-court visit than magistrates' court witnesses. This is probably because the Witness Service is more firmly established in the Crown Court. The Home Office is, however, funding the Witness Service to be available in all magistrates' courts. Full coverage is planned by April 2002. Almost a quarter of child witnesses had a visit to court before the date of the case (Table 2.4), compared with 9 per cent of adult witnesses. Twelve percent of victims, compared with 9 per cent of non-victims, had a pre-court visit.

Table 2.4: **Percentage of witnesses who had a pre-court visit and percentage aware they could have had a visit, by types of witnesses**

	Pre-court visit	Aware of visit
Witness type		
Victim	12	26
Other prosecution	9	26
Defence	8	13
Court type		
Crown	14	27
Magistrate	7	23
Sex		
Male	7	23
Female	13	26
Age		
Under 17	24	26
17–34	9	23
35–54	9	25
55+	8	31
Total	10	24

Base: All witnesses. Unweighted N=2496.
Notes: 1. Witnesses were only asked if they were aware that a visit was available to them if they did not report having had one.
2. Excludes 'don't knows'.

A third of sexual offence witnesses (35% for females and 22% for males) had a pre-trial visit compared with 8 per cent of witnesses of other offences. Women were more likely (for all offence types) to have had a pre-court visit.

Witnesses from social grades D and E (semi-skilled and unskilled) were more likely to have had a visit (15% and 13% respectively) than witnesses from grades A and B (professional and managerial) at 1 per cent and 9 per cent respectively. This could be related to education, with witnesses who are more educated being more confident and perhaps feeling less likely to need a visit. Also, among witnesses from social grade E there was a higher proportion of victim witnesses (43%) than from any other grade, and it can be seen in Table 2.4 that victims were more likely to have a pre-court visit than other witnesses. Three-fifths (60%) of witnesses from social grades D and E were witnesses to sexual or violent offences, and were more likely to have been told about pre-trial visits by the police, the Witness Service or Victim Support. Witnesses to such offences were also probably more likely to have requested a visit.

Of those who did not have a visit, prosecution witnesses were twice as likely as defence witnesses to be aware that a visit could be organised (26% compared with 13%). This could be due to the fact that the visits were organised by the Witness Service, and prosecution witnesses were more likely to have had contact with the Witness Service (54%) than defence witnesses (27%).

Satisfaction with the overall experience of being a witness was not linked with whether the witness actually had a pre-court visit. However, 81 per cent of witnesses who were aware that a visit could be organised were satisfied with their overall experience at court, compared with 74 per cent of those who were not aware.

Key Points

- Courteous treatment by the police was strongly linked with whether witnesses were satisfied overall with the police: 92 per cent of those treated courteously were satisfied, compared with only 30 per cent who were not treated courteously. Less than 10 per cent of witnesses felt that they were treated discourteously.

- 56 per cent of all witnesses said they were not kept informed at all by the police; the figure was lower – 44 per cent – for victim witnesses and higher – 61 per cent and 68 per cent – for other prosecution and defence witnesses. The police may not be entirely responsible, however, for contacting defence witnesses.

- 98 per cent of witnesses were satisfied with the police when they were kept regularly informed, compared with 83 per cent who were not kept informed at all.

- About a third (35%) of witnesses had contact with Victim Support.

- Over half of witnesses (56%) expressed concern about being a witness at court.

- Almost a quarter (23%) of victim witnesses were worried about meeting or seeing the defendant.

- Witnesses who felt they were given enough information about being a witness at court were more likely to feel satisfied with their overall experience at court than those who said they were given no information at all.

- Among the 56 per cent of witnesses who found the trial date convenient, overall satisfaction with the court experience was higher (82%) than among the 16 per cent of witnesses who found it very inconvenient (57%).

- The original date of the court case was changed for 39 per cent of witnesses.

- 1 in 10 witnesses, rising to a third of sexual offence witnesses, had a pre-trial visit.

3.   Witnesses' experiences at court

This chapter examines witnesses' experiences before, during and after giving evidence at court and their satisfaction levels at these different stages. It also looks at witnesses' overall satisfaction with their experience and their suggestions for improving the way witnesses are treated. Not all those who attended court gave evidence (60% did) but they were all asked about their treatment outside the courtroom.

Court staff

Most witnesses (85%) reported to reception on arriving at court for the first time. The majority (96%) were satisfied with their treatment by the court staff. The same percentage found the court staff courteous. Satisfaction with court staff was, however, lower among witnesses who were either not told or shown where to go on arrival at court or who found it unclear where they needed to go (87%, compared with 97% for those who were either shown or for whom it was clear where to go). However, it would appear that, by and large, court staff are helpful: 93 per cent of witnesses were told or shown where to go.

The Witness Service

The Witness Service (WS) is run by Victim Support. Trained volunteers supported by Witness Service staff deliver the service. They are present at all Crown Courts and some magistrates' courts.[19] Their role is to provide support and information to all witnesses, although defence witnesses tend to have less contact with them than prosecution witnesses. Witness Services are bound by the Victim's Charter standard, which tells victims/witnesses "you will be offered the support of the Witness Service at the Crown Court" (Victim Support Code of practice). Through the List of Witnesses Attending Court (LWAC) agreement between Victim Support and the CPS, all Crown Court Witness Services are supplied with an advance copy of the list of witnesses attending court in all cases where witnesses will be called.

Half of all witnesses had contact with the WS (see Table 3.1). A higher proportion of witnesses at the Crown Court had contact (74%) than at magistrates' courts (31%). This is likely to change over time when the WS becomes established in all magistrates' courts. The

---

19 Eventually, the Witness Service will cover all magistrates' courts. In April 2001 46 per cent were covered (unpublished data from the Home Office Justice and Victims Unit); full coverage is planned by the end of March 2002.

WS has grown already since the survey was conducted, and as such overall satisfaction may have already improved. The next survey will provide a better picture of this though, as the WS expansion programme is still in progress. WS contact was higher among white witnesses than among witnesses from ethnic minority groups. Several factors go some way to explaining this. Firstly, ethnic minority witnesses were more likely to be attending magistrates' courts (55% white; 63% Black; and 65% Asian) where there is less contact with the WS. Secondly, 77 per cent of Asian witnesses were male, and, as can be seen in Table 3.1, male witnesses had less contact than female witnesses. Lastly it might also be the case that witnesses from an ethnic minority were less likely to approach the WS. However, the sample size of ethnic minority witnesses was not large enough to explore this possibility.

Among those who had contact, the majority said that they were offered support and only 7 per cent said they had to ask for it. Among witnesses who had no contact with the WS, 37 per cent would have liked some support (47% of women and 30% of men). Over half (55%) of children who did not receive support would have liked to receive some. Whether or not witnesses had contact with the WS did not seem to be associated with overall satisfaction. However, for those witnesses who had contact, whether or not they were offered support was significant: witnesses who asked for, rather than being offered, support were less likely to feel satisfied overall. Among witnesses who did not have contact with the Witness Service, overall satisfaction was much lower among those who would have liked support (61%) than those who would not (82%). This suggests that contact with the WS for more witnesses could well be beneficial in terms of raising overall satisfaction.

Table 3.1: **Contact with the Witness Service, and whether support was wanted, by witness types (percentages)**

	Contact with WS	Whether would have liked support
Witness type		
Victim	50	53
Other prosecution	56	29
Defence	27	37
Court type		
Crown	74	39
Magistrate	31	37
Sex		
Male	48	30
Female	53	47
Age		
Under 17	46	55
17–34	49	38
35–54	54	37
55+	46	24
Ethnicity		
White	52	36
Black	43	56
Asian	35	47
Other	44	43
Total	51	37

Base: All witnesses. Unweighted N=2430.
Notes: 1. All witnesses were asked whether they had contact with the WS. Witnesses who did not were asked whether they would have liked support.
2. Excludes 'don't knows'.

Initially, it is perhaps surprising that more child witnesses did not have support from the WS. A possible explanation might be that child witnesses had more contact with Victim Support before court, and were assumed to have less need of support on the day of the court case. In fact, the proportion of child and adult witnesses who reported contact with Victim Support were virtually the same[20] and witnesses who had contact with Victim Support were actually

---

20 33 per cent of child witnesses and 34 per cent of adult witnesses reported contact with Victim Support.

more likely to report contact with the Witness Service.[21] This is not surprising when it is considered that it is Victim Support's policy to contact the WS once it is known that a victim or witness will be attending court. The reason that child witnesses were less likely to have WS support is probably because child/young witnesses are more likely to be accompanied to court than others (for example, by parents or specialist police officers) and, as a result, the WS may be less likely to see them as needing support. This does not reflect WS policy: the service provided to children by the Crown Court Witness Service is governed by the same principles as the service for adults (Victim Support Code of Practice).

It should be noted that Victim Support Schemes do not deal with cases of child abuse covered by statutory procedures, whereas the Witness Service does. There is therefore a group of young witnesses who may receive Witness Service support, whom one would not expect to have received contact with Victim Support. In respect of young people who do not receive Witness Service support, Victim Support is in the process of negotiating a referral agreement, which would ensure referrals at the stage of plea and direction hearings, in order to ensure that every young witness is offered the service.

Of those who had contact, 93 per cent felt that the Witness Service was able to offer support, regardless of age, sex or court type. Most witnesses had contact with the WS on the day they came to court, but 15 per cent had contact before the day.

The WS can provide support to witnesses at three different stages: whilst they wait to give evidence, whilst they are in the courtroom (for instance being available to accompany the witness into the room) and after giving evidence. The survey found that of witnesses assisted by the WS, 92 per cent received support whilst they were waiting, regardless of witness type, court type, sex or age. A quarter of witnesses received support in the courtroom and 40 per cent after giving evidence (Table A3.1 in Appendix). Support was less uniformly spread at these latter two stages. Crown Court witnesses were more likely to receive support both in the courtroom and after giving evidence than magistrates' courts witnesses. Women were more likely to receive support (32% in the courtroom and 49% after giving evidence) than men (18% and 31% respectively). Witnesses were also more likely to receive support in the courtroom and after giving evidence if they were witnesses of a sexual or violent offence. Women were more likely than men to be the victims of such offences and this is one factor in explaining the greater levels of assistance provided to women by the WS.

---

21 67 per cent of those who reported contact with Victim Support said they also had contact with the WS, compared with 39 per cent of witnesses who did not have contact with Victim Support.

Pre-trial visits to court

Overall, 48 per cent of witnesses (51% prosecution and 31% defence) either were given the opportunity to look round one of the courtrooms before the case began or had had a previous familiarisation visit to court before the day of the trial (Table A3.2 in Appendix). Half of Crown Court witnesses were given the opportunity before the case began compared with 37 per cent of magistrates' court witnesses. A further 5 per cent of witnesses at the Crown Court had already had a visit before the day of the case. Child witnesses were more likely to have had a look round a courtroom (65%) than adult witnesses (47%).

Waiting to give evidence

Time spent waiting

Table 3.2 shows defence witnesses said that they had to wait significantly longer to give evidence than victims. This is probably determined by the fact that prosecution witnesses give evidence before defence witnesses in criminal cases. Victim witnesses had to wait less time than other prosecution witnesses. Victim witnesses are usually key witnesses and therefore often likely to be called before non-victim prosecution witnesses. A third of defence witnesses and 17 per cent of other prosecution witnesses said that they had to wait longer than four hours, whereas only 9 per cent of victims had to wait that long.

There were marked differences between magistrates' courts and the Crown Court. At magistrates' courts, 37 per cent of witnesses said they were called within one hour, and only 12 per cent had to wait longer than four hours. In contrast, at the Crown Court less than a quarter of witnesses said that they were called within one hour and a quarter waited longer than four hours before giving evidence. This is generally consistent with the latest *Joint Performance Management Witness Survey* (November 2000)[22] which found that at the Crown Court just over half of witnesses (52%) had to wait for two hours or more to give evidence and 50 per cent of witnesses in magistrates' courts had to wait one hour or more.

Differences in the kinds of case dealt with in the two courts probably explain these patterns. In particular, Crown Court cases are likely to be longer, more complex, and involve lengthier cross-examination. These factors make it more difficult to say with precision when a particular witness may be called into court to give their evidence.

---

22 The latest survey showed that 46 per cent of witnesses in the Crown Court and 53 per cent of witnesses in magistrates' courts were released without giving evidence. Average waiting times were 2 hours 38 minutes for the Crown Court and 1 hour 27 minutes for magistrates' courts. Waiting times in the Crown Court have decreased since the first monitoring survey in 1997 from 3 hours 2 minutes, whilst they have remained roughly the same in magistrates' courts (1 hour 30 minutes in 1997).

Table 3.2: **How long witnesses said they had to wait before giving evidence (percentages)**

	Up to 1 hour	Up to 2 hours	Up to 4 hours	Longer than 4 hours
Witness type				
Victim	43	28	19	9
Other prosecution	29	31	22	17
Defence	17	24	25	34
Court type				
Crown	23	25	27	25
Magistrate	37	33	18	12
Total	31	29	22	17

Base: All witnesses who gave evidence. Unweighted N=1483.
Note: Excludes 'don't knows'.

Views about how long they should expect to wait to give evidence varied among witnesses, depending on whether they had been a victim or not. Over half (57%) of victims thought it was reasonable to wait for only up to an hour before going into the courtroom to give evidence, compared with 42 per cent of non-victims. This may be because waiting to give evidence is more daunting or worrying for victims, due to concerns about seeing the defendant, and general anxieties relating both to the trial and to the offence itself. Crown Court and magistrates' court witnesses also differed in what they thought was a reasonable length of time to wait. Just over a third (36%) of Crown Court witnesses thought that they should expect to be called within an hour, compared with more than half (55%) of those at magistrates' courts. Witnesses at the Crown Court are likely to be aware that the case could last for some times, and that there may be several witnesses giving evidence in the same case. They might well have been told to expect to wait longer than one hour.

Expectations also varied with age. Thus, about a quarter (26%) of witnesses aged 55+ felt that it was reasonable to wait for either longer than four hours or 'as long as it took'. Only 7 per cent of child witnesses thought this, with the majority (65%) feeling that it was only reasonable to wait for up to an hour.

Satisfaction

Waiting to give evidence was linked with overall satisfaction: 77 per cent of witnesses who waited for under four hours were satisfied, compared with 65 per cent of those who had to wait for longer than this. Among witnesses who were given no information about what was going on whilst waiting at court, and who had to wait longer than four hours to be called, overall satisfaction was only 44 per cent.[23]

Satisfaction was also linked with witnesses' expectations. Those who felt that it was reasonable to wait for 'as long as it takes' were more likely to feel satisfied with their overall experience (86%), compared with witnesses who felt it was only reasonable to wait up to an hour (73%). This suggests that giving witnesses more information before arrival at court and during their wait to explain possible delays could be beneficial.

Just over a fifth (22%) of witnesses said they were given no information at all about what was going on whilst they were waiting at court. Forty-five per cent said they were informed at least once an hour, 14 per cent once an hour and 14 per cent less than once an hour. Six per cent said they were not waiting long enough to need an update. Of those informed once an hour or less often only 62 per cent were subsequently satisfied with their overall experience, compared with 82 per cent of those who were informed at least once an hour about what was happening.

Separate waiting rooms for prosecution and defence witnesses

Almost three-quarters (73%) of prosecution and defence witnesses were put in separate waiting rooms. Child witnesses were more likely to wait in separate areas (83%) than adult witnesses (73%). This is unsurprising, especially since separating witnesses is one of the special measures introduced for vulnerable and intimidated witnesses, who include children (*Speaking up for Justice*, 1998).

It might have been thought that facilities would more often be available in the Crown Court to separate witnesses. However, court type made no significant difference: 76 per cent of witnesses at the Crown Court were put in separate waiting rooms, compared with 72 per cent of witnesses at magistrates' courts.

Separation of prosecution and defence witnesses was only weakly associated with overall satisfaction, with 78 per cent of witnesses who were put in separate waiting rooms feeling satisfied, compared with 71 per cent of witnesses who were not separated. In *Speaking up for Justice*, the Statement of National Standards of Witness Care affirms that, where possible, there should be separate waiting accommodation for prosecution and defence witnesses. However, in some courts it is impossible to separate witnesses due to the physical layout of the building. It has been suggested that alternative approaches should be adopted when this is the case, such as the use of pagers (*Speaking up for Justice*, 1998).

---

23 This is consistent with Plotnikoff and Woolfson's (1997) qualitative research which highlighted complaints about waiting times at court, as well as worries about seeing the defendant and about not understanding what was happening in court, and the need for more information.

In the court room

Three out of every five witnesses who attended court to give evidence actually ended up doing so. Of the 40 per cent who did not give evidence, the main reason was because the defendant pleaded guilty at a late stage. Overall satisfaction was not related to whether witnesses gave evidence or not.

Satisfaction levels with the different individuals involved in the courtroom process (prosecution barristers/CPS lawyers, defence lawyers, judges and magistrates) varied considerably. Table 3.3 shows that satisfaction with judges and magistrates was particularly high for all witnesses. Typically, however, judges and magistrates will have only limited contact with witnesses.

Unsurprisingly, defence witnesses were not as satisfied with their treatment by the CPS/prosecution lawyer as prosecution witnesses, and prosecution witnesses (especially victims) were less satisfied with their treatment by defence lawyers. Satisfaction with defence lawyers was higher among male witnesses than female witnesses. This might be because female witnesses were more likely to be witnesses or victims of a sexual or violent offence (57%) than men (48%) and therefore to find the cross-examination process more upsetting. Satisfaction with defence lawyers was lower for witnesses, both male and female, of a sexual or violent offence (63%) than other offences (72%).

Witnesses' satisfaction with defence lawyers appears to increase with age. However, in part this is due to the fact that defence witnesses were under-represented among younger age groups: thus, only 4 per cent of witnesses under 17 were defence witnesses (compared with 51% being victims and 45% being other prosecution witnesses). It is also strongly related to the fact that the majority of child witnesses (81%) were witnesses of a sexual or violent offence, and over half were victims. Young witnesses and victims of these offences are particularly likely to have found questioning by defence lawyers about the details of the offence upsetting.

Whether the witness was cross-examined in the courtroom affected satisfaction levels with both prosecution and defence lawyers, and also overall satisfaction (see Table 3.4). Witnesses who were not cross-examined were significantly more likely to feel satisfied. The impact of cross-examination varied according to whether the witness was appearing for the defence or the prosecution, with the latter being less likely to be satisfied. Thus, 68 per cent of defence witnesses who were cross-examined felt satisfied with the prosecution lawyer, compared with 61 per cent of prosecution witnesses in relation to the defence lawyer.

Table 3.3: Satisfaction with courtroom personnel, by witness type (percentages)

	CPS/prosecution lawyer	Defence lawyer	Judge/ magistrate
Witness type			
Victim	82	45	92
Other prosecution	92	69	97
Defence	68	92	95
Court type			
Crown	86	69	96
Magistrate	88	65	95
Sex			
Male	87	70	94
Female	86	63	96
Age			
Under 17	90	40	97
17–34	88	65	95
35–54	84	69	95
55+	90	85	95
Total	87	67	95

Base: All who had contact with the three agencies/groups. Unweighted N=1788 for CPS/prosecution lawyers; N=1354 for defence lawyers; and N=1442 for judges/magistrates.

Notes: 1. Percentages are those 'fairly' or 'very' satisfied with the way the above personnel treated the witness in court.

2. Excludes 'don't knows'.

Table 3.4: *Percentage of witnesses saying they were very/fairly happy with their treatment overall and with lawyers, by whether they were cross-examined*

	Cross-examined	Not cross-examined
Overall satisfaction	74	83
Satisfaction with prosecution lawyer	68	94
Satisfaction with defence lawyer	61	95

Base: All witnesses who gave evidence. Unweighted N=1489.
Notes: 1. Excludes 'don't knows'.
        2. The proportion of those cross-examined who were satisfied with prosecution lawyers related to defence witnesses only; the figure for those cross-examined who were satisfied with defence lawyers relates only to prosecution witnesses.

Over 90 per cent of all witnesses felt they were treated courteously by the lawyer representing 'their side'[24] of the case.

The majority of witnesses (82%) felt that the lawyer for their 'own side' gave them both the opportunity to say everything they wanted to when being questioned and also treated them courteously.

Witnesses felt that they were not treated as well by the 'other side's' lawyer. Only 45 per cent of victims felt they were treated courteously. The figure for non-victims was 66 per cent (Table A3.3 in Appendix). Perhaps it is inevitable in an adversarial system, in which the evidence presented by one side is robustly challenged by the other side, that those who are at the receiving end of cross-examination should feel unhappy at styles of questioning which may suggest that they are not believed. Male witnesses were more likely to feel they were treated courteously (64%) than female witnesses (55%). Just under half of all witnesses (48%) felt that the lawyer both gave them the opportunity to say everything they wanted to and also treated them courteously. Over a quarter (28%) of witnesses felt that the 'other side's' lawyer neither treated them courteously nor gave them the opportunity to say everything they wanted to. Reports by witnesses of courteous treatment increased with age, as did perceptions that they were given the opportunity to say everything. Possibly lawyers show greater sensitivity towards older witnesses.

24 'Own side's' lawyer refers to CPS/prosecution for prosecution witnesses, and defence lawyers for defence witnesses. It should be recognised that the CPS acts on behalf of the Crown, not on behalf of individual victims. However, this concept is not easy to convey to witnesses during the course of a survey interview and the liberty was therefore taken of referring to CPS lawyers as the lawyer 'for their side' when questioning prosecution witnesses.

Satisfaction with lawyers was substantially greater if witnesses felt they were treated courteously and given the opportunity to say everything they wanted. Overall satisfaction was also associated with treatment by lawyers in the courtroom (Table 3.5). Among witnesses who were treated courteously by both sides and were given the opportunity to say everything by both sides, 89 per cent felt satisfied overall.

Overall satisfaction among witnesses who were cross-examined varied significantly, depending on whether they felt that they were treated courteously. About three-quarters (76%) of victim witnesses and 86 per cent of non-victims felt satisfied when treated courteously (compared with 50% of victims and 67% of non-victims who felt they were not treated courteously).

The way in which witnesses were treated by the 'other side's' lawyer had a greater impact on overall satisfaction than treatment by the lawyer from the witnesses' 'side'. Perhaps witnesses were less likely to expect courteous treatment from the 'other side's' lawyer, and so when they were treated courteously it had more of an effect.

Table 3.5:   Overall satisfaction by treatment in the courtroom (percentages)

	Overall satisfaction
Whether treated courteously by own sides' lawyer	
Yes	77
No	47
Whether given opportunity to say everything by own side's lawyer	
Yes	82
No	43
Whether treated courteously by other side's lawyer	
Yes	84
No	60
Whether given opportunity to say everything by other side's lawyer	
Yes	86
No	56
Total	74

Base: All witnesses who gave evidence. Unweighted N=1489.
Note: Excludes 'don't knows'.

After giving evidence

Leaving the court

After testifying, 89 per cent of witnesses were allowed to go straight home, the remainder being asked to stay at court longer. Over half (52%) of all witnesses (46% of victims) were not told what would happen next. For some witnesses this would not be a problem, but for others – especially victims who might want information about the verdict and further support – it could be rather frustrating and even concerning. Among the 11 per cent of witnesses who were asked to stay at court rather than being able to go straight home, 37 per cent were not given an explanation of why. Witnesses who were allowed to go straight home were more likely to feel satisfied with their overall experience (77%) than those who had to stay at court longer (65%).

Follow-up support

Sixteen percent of witnesses said that they were provided with details of follow-up support, 76 per cent were not, and a further 7 per cent felt it was not needed. Among the three-quarters of witnesses who did not receive support details, 32 per cent would have liked to. The wish for further support was higher among victims, at 50 per cent. Among witnesses who did not receive support, overall satisfaction was substantially lower for those who would have liked support (61%) than those who would not (81%). The WS was the agency which most often provided details of the available follow-up support (43%). The findings would seem to suggest that providing further assistance to all who wanted it would be an important way of raising satisfaction with the experience of being a witness.

Verdict

Overall, 64 per cent of witnesses who knew the outcome of the case thought that a fair verdict was reached. Non-victims were more likely than victims to think the verdict was fair. A greater proportion of witnesses from magistrates' courts said they believed the verdict to be fair (69%) than witnesses from the Crown Court (59%). This may reflect the higher conviction rate in the magistrates' courts than in the Crown Court.[25]

Overall satisfaction was related to whether or not the witness thought the verdict of the case was fair, with 86 per cent of witnesses being satisfied when they thought the outcome was fair, compared with 57 per cent of those who thought it to be unfair.

---

25 In 1999 about 76 per cent of those tried in the Crown Court were convicted compared with around 98 per cent of those cases dealt with by magistrates' courts (calculated from figures in Criminal Statistics 1999 Supplementary Tables Vols 1 and 2).

Not surprisingly, victims were unlikely to think that a fair verdict was reached unless the defendant was convicted. Satisfaction among prosecution witnesses generally was low if the defendant was acquitted and, conversely, high among defence witnesses.

Satisfaction was lowest among prosecution witnesses when the case was dropped before the hearing got under way (Table 3.6). This is unsurprising, as it would mean these witnesses did not get the chance to give evidence. Having come to court ready to act as a witness and to act on behalf of the prosecution, it could leave witnesses feeling that their evidence had not been regarded as being of any significance.

Table 3.6: *Overall satisfaction and attitude towards fairness of verdict, by verdict and witness type (percentages)*

	Overall satisfaction		Whether thought verdict was fair	
	Prosecution	Defence	Prosecution	Defence
Defendant pleaded guilty	82	74	75	61
Defendant found guilty after trial	81	64	83	39
Defendant acquitted after trial	59	90	15	83
Prosecution dropped case before hearing started	51	75	32	92
Case collapsed after hearing started	60	82	17	75
Don't know	73	80	65	63

Base: All witnesses. Unweighted N=2498.

Witness expenses

The majority of witnesses (85%) said they were given a witness expenses claim form – 90 per cent of prosecution witnesses but only 49 per cent of defence witnesses. The CPS deals with the expenses of their witnesses. On request the court will hand out witness expenses claim forms to defence witnesses, but not all are eligible – for instance those who are character witnesses. Crown Court witnesses were more likely to say that they had received a form than magistrates' court witnesses (91% compared with 81%). Among witnesses who had already received their expenses, 76 per cent said it covered all of their costs. These witnesses were more likely to have been satisfied overall (81%) compared with those for whom the expenses did not cover all costs (64%).

Intimidation at court

Witnesses were asked whether at any point in the process of going to court to give evidence they felt intimidated, either by an individual or by the process/environment as a whole. Substantial numbers reported feelings of intimidation, with 25 per cent feeling intimidated by an individual and 18 per cent by the process. Five per cent of witnesses felt intimidated by both an individual and by the process as a whole. Table 3.7 examines how the experience of intimidation varied according to the characteristics of witnesses.

Victims, females and children were the most likely to report feelings of intimidation by an individual. For example, 47 per cent of under-17 year olds reported feeling intimidated. The 1998 British Crime Survey (Tarling, Dowds and Budd, 2000) also found that female victims were more likely to feel intimidated than men. Feelings of intimidation by the process were more uniformly spread. Overall, 39 per cent of witnesses felt intimidated by either an individual or the process as a whole, or both. This was much higher among child witnesses, at 57 per cent.

Satisfaction was associated with whether witnesses reported feelings of intimidation. Figure 3.1 below shows that among witnesses who felt intimidated by both an individual and by the process as a whole, satisfaction was low, at 39 per cent. Witnesses who felt intimidated by an individual only were more likely to feel satisfied than those who felt intimidated only by the process. Eighty-four per cent of witnesses who did not report any feelings of intimidation felt satisfied with their overall experience at court.

Table 3.7:   Intimidation by witness type, court, gender and age (percentages)

	By individual & process	By individual only	By process only	Neither
Witness type				
Victim	8	28	15	49
Other prosecution	3	18	13	66
Defence	4	16	12	68
Court type				
Crown	5	19	15	61
Magistrate	5	22	12	62
Sex				
Male	3	17	12	68
Female	7	24	15	53
Age				
Under 17	9	38	10	43
17–34	6	21	15	58
35–54	4	18	13	64
55+	1	15	10	75
Total	5	21	13	61

Base: All witnesses. Unweighted N=2492.
Note: Excludes 'don't knows'.

Figure 3.1:   Percentage of witnesses very or fairly satisfied with their overall experience at court, by whether they felt intimidated

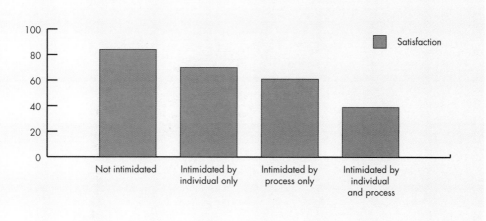

When asked what it was about the process of giving evidence or the court environment that made the witness feel intimidated, a number of factors were mentioned. The most common were:

- daunting environment/court (19%);

- lawyer intimidating or rude (18%);

- no knowledge about what would happen in court (17%);

- too close to defendant in the court (13%);

- defence and prosecution in same areas (11%);

- all eyes in court upon me (10%).

There are limits to how far these factors can be addressed – for instance, all eyes being on the witness – other than clearing the court of spectators. And making significant changes to the court environment would be an expensive option. However, giving witnesses more information about the court process, and making more of an effort to separate prosecution and defence witnesses, are viable options which may help alleviate some of these feelings of intimidation. Similarly the process of being cross-examined will always be a daunting one and only so much can be done to ease this. However, lawyers should adhere to their professional bodies' codes of conduct: whether any further action can be taken is a matter for the Bar Council and Law Society to consider.

Intimidation by an individual was felt at several different stages of being a witness. Some witnesses felt intimidated at more than one stage. As Table 3.8 shows, witnesses were more likely to feel intimidated at court (whilst waiting/giving evidence) than before or after.

Table 3.8:   Witness intimidation by an individual (percentages)

	Percent feeling intimidated
Before the case came to court	35
Whilst waiting to give evidence	49
Whilst giving evidence	47
After giving evidence but still at court	15
After leaving court	17

Base: All witnesses who felt intimidated by an individual. Unweighted N=623.
Note: Witnesses could mention feeling intimidated at more than one stage.

By far the most commonly stated source of intimidation was the defendant (49% among witnesses generally, and 58% among victims). Just over a fifth (22%) of intimidated witnesses said they felt intimidated by the defendant's family or friends. About a third (34%) mentioned an official of some sort as being the source of the intimidation (including police, lawyers, court staff, judges and magistrates), although lawyers were the most commonly mentioned (28%). Looking only at witnesses who were actually required to give evidence, 39 per cent mentioned a lawyer as the source of the intimidation. What witnesses interpret as intimidation is not necessarily what criminal justice officials would interpret as such. For instance, it would not be expected that lawyers might potentially threaten or be violent towards a witness, whereas a defendant might. However, the demeanour of lawyers may nonetheless be overbearing or intimidating.

Witnesses who were cross-examined in the court-room were more likely to report feelings of intimidation – 32 per cent by an individual and 21 per cent by the process. This compares with 15 per cent of witnesses who were not cross-examined feeling intimidated by an individual and 14 per cent by the process. Among those who were cross-examined and who felt intimidated by an individual, 41 per cent named a lawyer as the source. As mentioned above (p.38), the process of being cross-examined is always going to be a daunting one. Among witnesses who said they felt intimidated by the process as a whole, 26 per cent mentioned finding a lawyer intimidating or rude (this was lower, at 7 per cent, among witnesses who were not cross-examined) and 10 per cent said they were made to feel guilty of something. Among witnesses who were cross-examined, 47 per cent said they were intimidated, compared with 27 per cent of witnesses not cross-examined. Feeling intimidated by a lawyer can be included in both personal and process intimidation. Taking this into account, overall, 10 per cent of witnesses surveyed said that lawyers were the source of their intimidation.

Intimidation and courteous treatment were linked. Thus, when witnesses felt that the 'other side's' lawyer did not treat them courteously, half also felt intimidated by an individual, compared with 20 per cent of those treated courteously. This again could be related to the possibility that witnesses may feel daunted or uncomfortable if they are not treated in the way they were expecting. Twelve per cent of witnesses who said they were not treated courteously felt intimidated by both an individual and the process, compared with only 3 per cent who felt they were treated courteously. There was a similar greater likelihood of witnesses feeling intimidated by the process and an individual where they felt they were not given the opportunity to say everything they wanted to when being questioned by the lawyer for the other side.

Among witnesses who felt intimidated by an individual, under half (42%) reported this intimidation, in the majority of cases to the police (63%). The WS was also told about 18 per cent (of reported incidences), CPS/lawyers about 17 per cent, and the Court Service about 13 per cent. In cases where intimidation is drawn to the attention of the court, the course of action would depend on the circumstance and context of the intimidation. Court staff would refer any incident of witness intimidation to the judge or magistrate. There may be occasions when the judge or magistrate asks for such an occurrence to be reported to the police. Most likely, however, would be that the witness would be advised by the court to report the matter to the police, maybe with the assistance of the Witness Service. If intimidation is occurring, the Witness Service would be expected to take action with the witness's agreement. In rare cases, some action could be necessary without consent, for instance if the safety of others was being compromised. This could be in the form of calling security to protect other court users. CPS action regarding intimidation would depend on the time and place the complaint is made and the nature and seriousness of the complaint. If information came to the CPS outside court, the witness would either be referred to the police or the lawyer concerned would contact the police and ask for the matter to be investigated. Only 4 per cent of witnesses who reported intimidation told Victim Support about it. However, Victim Support is not usually represented at court, and most of the intimidation reported was before or while giving evidence. Crown Court witnesses were more likely to have reported the intimidation than magistrates' court witnesses. The group most likely to report feelings of intimidation were witnesses aged 35–54 (50%). It may be that intimidation is more an accepted fact of life among younger witnesses, or they might feel that nothing would be done even if they did report it. Older witnesses may have been more shocked by the intimidation and therefore more likely to report it.

Almost half (47%) of witnesses who reported feelings of intimidation felt that it was dealt with effectively. Overall satisfaction and satisfaction with police and CPS/prosecution was linked with whether or not the reported intimidation was felt to have been dealt with effectively. Thus, 57 per cent of witnesses were dissatisfied overall if the reported intimidation had not been effectively dealt with. Satisfaction with both the police and with the CPS/prosecution was also significantly lowered (36% were dissatisfied with the police and 32% with the CPS/prosecution when reported intimidation was not felt to be dealt with effectively).

Improvements

Witnesses were asked, unprompted, for their suggestions about what improvements, if any, could be made to the whole process of being a witness. A wide range of ideas were put forward, the most common of which were:

- more information should be given to witnesses prior to arriving in court (15%)

- prosecution and defence parties should be kept separate (14%)

- more information and help should be given by the police and CPS during the case (8%)

- waiting times in court should be reduced (6%)

Other suggestions included more notice of trial dates or changes in dates, and also more information about the outcome of the case. Witnesses mentioning the top four improvements listed above were less satisfied overall with their experience at court. For example 60 per cent of witnesses who mentioned wanting more information from the police/CPS during the case felt satisfied, compared with 75 per cent of those not mentioning it. Witnesses who said there were no improvements to be made were very likely to feel satisfied (93%) compared with 73 per cent of those who mentioned any improvement.

Key Points

- 98 per cent of witnesses were satisfied with their treatment by court staff

- Half of all witnesses had contact with the Witness Service, and 90 per cent of these witnesses felt the WS was able to offer support

- 37 per cent of those who did not have contact would have liked some support

- Almost half (47%) of witnesses (increasing to 64% of child witnesses) were given the opportunity to look round a courtroom before the case began

- Almost a fifth (17%) of witnesses had to wait longer than 4 hours before giving evidence

- Waiting to give evidence was associated with overall satisfaction: 77 per cent of witnesses waiting 4 hours or less were satisfied, compared with 65 per cent of witnesses waiting longer than 4 hours

- Almost three-quarters (74%) of prosecution and defence witnesses were put in separate waiting rooms

- Witnesses who were cross-examined were less likely to feel satisfied overall and with prosecution and defence lawyers

- Witnesses who were treated courteously by lawyers, and given the opportunity to say everything they wanted to when being questioned, were more likely to feel satisfied

- 16 per cent of witnesses were provided with details of follow-up support. Almost a third of witnesses who did not receive follow-up support would have liked some

- Overall, 64 per cent of witnesses thought that a fair verdict was reached in their case

- 86 per cent of witnesses who thought a fair verdict had been reached were satisfied, compared with 57 per cent of those who thought the verdict to be unfair

- A quarter of witnesses felt intimidated by an individual and 18 per cent by the process

- Intimidation was higher among victims, females and children

- Satisfaction was strongly associated with intimidation

4.   Factors affecting satisfaction

Chapters 2 and 3 examined a range of factors that were associated with witnesses' satisfaction with their experience at court. This chapter takes this analysis further by seeking to identify those factors which are most important in determining satisfaction with their experience of the criminal justice system as a whole. The chapter also provides information about witnesses' willingness to act as a witness again and reports the results of a similar analysis to identify the factors which predict willingness. In addition, the chapter also presents the results of questions designed to establish witnesses' confidence in the criminal justice system. First, however, it looks at overall satisfaction and how this varied according to the type of witness.

Overall satisfaction

Just over three-quarters (76%) of witnesses said they were very or fairly satisfied with their overall experience. Table A4.1 shows that overall satisfaction varied considerably between victims and other witnesses. Thus, 67 per cent of victims were satisfied compared with 80 per cent of other prosecution witnesses and 77 per cent of defence witnesses. Differences between one kind of witness and another were less noticeable in relation to satisfaction with specific criminal justice agencies, although (as was discussed in chapter 3) prosecution witnesses tended to be far less satisfied with defence lawyers and defence witnesses tended to be less satisfied with their treatment by prosecution lawyers. Age, sex and court type (i.e. magistrates' or Crown) were not strongly linked with satisfaction. The number of witnesses from ethnic minority backgrounds was too small to say whether or not ethnic origin was associated with satisfaction.

Predicting dissatisfaction

In order to explore which factors were most strongly and independently associated with overall satisfaction, the statistical technique of logistic regression was used. Using this technique it was possible to build a model which predicts dissatisfaction. In practice some models are more accurate than others, but this method provides an indication of how accurate (i.e. how good at predicting dissatisfaction) each model is, and how much each factor contributes. It should be noted that one factor may represent several factors found to be related to satisfaction in earlier chapters. There was a high degree of inter-correlation and it did not make sense to enter each of them into the model separately. One version of the model examined all witnesses, while other versions looked only at those who were actually required to give evidence and those who were not required to give evidence. The accuracy of the models to predict dissatisfaction was around the 81/82 per cent mark accurate. The models were designed to predict dissatisfaction rather than satisfaction for two main reasons. Firstly, to increase satisfaction rates it is important to look at why people are dissatisfied. Secondly, given that most people are satisfied, it makes sense to try to identify why some people are different. Satisfaction with each individual agency was not included in the models because not all witnesses were asked about each agency. Some, for example, might have had no contact with Victim Support or the Witness Service. However, there are indications that the level of satisfaction with individual agencies did have an effect on overall satisfaction.

All witnesses

The verdict and intimidation were the strongest predictors of dissatisfaction (Table A4.4). The odds of feeling dissatisfied were over four times higher for witnesses who thought that an unfair verdict was reached or for witnesses who felt intimidated by both an individual and the process as a whole. Convenience of court date and satisfaction with the facilities at court also exert a strong influence. Witnesses who found the date very inconvenient or who were not satisfied with the facilities at court were more likely to feel dissatisfied. The amount of advance information given to witnesses about what would happen at court, as well as the frequency of being kept informed whilst waiting to give evidence, were also significant predictors. Witnesses given no information whilst waiting were twice as likely to feel dissatisfied as those informed at least once an hour.

Witnesses who gave evidence

Not all witnesses were required to give evidence. For those who did, intimidation and perceived fairness of the verdict are even stronger predictors of dissatisfaction (Table A4.5). The odds of feeling dissatisfied were 6.5 times higher for witnesses who felt intimidated by both an individual and the process as a whole. It was noted above that the provision of information was an important predictive factor of dissatisfaction among witnesses generally. However, when looking only at witnesses who gave evidence, this was no longer so important. A new factor emerged as significant, namely the treatment by the lawyer 'on the side of' the witness. For example, witnesses were more likely to feel dissatisfied if they felt that 'their' lawyer did not give them the opportunity to say everything they wanted to when being questioned in court. Being a victim witness increased the likelihood of dissatisfaction by almost 2.5 times.

Witnesses who did not give evidence

For those witnesses who came to court to give evidence but were not called, intimidation, information and convenience of court date remained strong predictors (Table A4.6). Not knowing the verdict, and for those who did know it, feeling it was unfair, were also important. For those who did not know the verdict, the odds of feeling dissatisfied with the overall experience increased almost four-fold. Negative views about the standard of court facilities and the provision of information were also strong predictors of dissatisfaction.

Willingness to be a witness again

Three out of five witnesses (61%) said they would be happy to be a witness again.[26] Victims and defence witnesses were markedly less likely than other prosecution witnesses to say they would be happy to testify again (Table 4.1). They were also less likely to say they were satisfied with their overall experience. This was more marked among victim witnesses, however. Although gender was not related to witness satisfaction, males were significantly more likely than females to say they would be happy to be a witness again. Child witnesses were the least likely to say they would be happy. Whether the respondent had been a witness before was also relevant, with a higher proportion of those who had previously been witnesses saying they would be very or fairly happy to act as a witness again. This may reflect a greater sense of public spiritedness among some members of the population (or even that some may enjoy being a witness). In addition, those who have been witnesses before know more about what to expect, and so may be more likely to agree to be one again.

Willingness to be a witness again increased with age, which could be related to feelings of greater social responsibility among the older generation. The first national Citizenship Survey, currently being conducted, is exploring public perceptions of such responsibilities in more detail.

The proportion of witnesses who said they would be happy to be a witness again (61%) may be contrasted with the rather higher proportion who said they were very or fairly satisfied with their overall experience (76%). It seems that a positive experience as a witness does not necessarily translate into wanting to repeat that experience. Thus, just over a fifth of witnesses (21%) said they were satisfied with their experience, but would not want to be a witness again in another trial (Table 4.2). Just over half (55%) of witnesses said that they were both satisfied with their experience at court and would be happy to be a witness again. However, the proportion was significantly lower among child witnesses, with only 39 per cent saying they were both satisfied and happy.

---

26 Southgate and Grosvenor's (2000) study also found some reluctance on the part of the general public to become involved as a witness in a court case.

Over a third of child witnesses (36%) said they were satisfied with their overall experience, but they would not be happy to be a witness again. Southgate and Grosvenor (2000) also carried out a small-scale qualitative survey to explore the kinds of things that are related to confidence in the CJS, which covered different users of the CJS.

Female witnesses (27%) and defence witnesses (also 27%) were both more likely than average to be satisfied with their experience as a witness but unhappy about acting as a witness again. About a fifth (18%) of witnesses said they were both dissatisfied with their experience as a witness and would not be happy to be a witness again. The figure was highest among victim witnesses, at 25 per cent. A very small proportion of witnesses (6%) were dissatisfied with their experience of being a witness but said they would be happy to be a witness again. Possibly, feelings of public spiritedness overcame their negative feelings about their recent experiences at court.

Table 4.1: ***Percentage of witnesses saying they would be very/fairly happy to be a witness again***

	Happy to be a witness again
Witness type	
Victim	53
Other prosecution	66
Defence	56
Court type	
Crown	60
Magistrates'	62
Sex	
Male	67
Female	54
Age	
Under 17	42
17–34	59
35–54	65
55+	67
Whether been a witness before	
Yes	68
No	59
Total	61

Base: All witnesses. Unweighted N=2406.
Note: Excludes 'don't knows'.

Table 4.2: **Overall satisfaction and happiness to be a witness again, by witness type (percentages)**

	Satisfied and happy	Satisfied but not happy	Dissatisfied but happy	Dissatisfied and not happy
Witness type				
Victim	45	22	8	25
Other prosecution	61	20	6	14
Defence	50	27	6	18
Sex				
Male	59	17	7	16
Female	49	27	5	19
Age group				
Child	39	36	4	21
Adult	56	20	6	18
Total	55	21	6	18

Base: All witnesses. Unweighted N=2355.
Note: Excludes 'don't knows'.

Predicting unwillingness to be a witness again

As with overall satisfaction, a logistic regression analysis was carried out to identify which factors, after controlling for the effect of other variables, were significantly associated with preparedness to be a witness again. For the same reasons outlined above in relation to dissatisfaction, the model was designed to predict unwillingness rather than willingness to act as a witness again. The accuracy of the model to predict unwillingness was 71 per cent. Verdict is again a strong predictor of unwillingness to be a witness again, but is not as powerful a factor as it was for predicting dissatisfaction (Table A4.7). Intimidation remains the strongest predictor. Convenience of court date and satisfaction with court facilities are important. The status of the witness is also relevant. Thus, child witnesses are more likely than adults to be unwilling to be a witness again. Females and victim and defence witnesses are also less likely than males and other prosecution witnesses, but these variables had only a relatively small influence.

Satisfaction and happiness to be a witness again

Table A4.8 looks at the way in which verdict, intimidation, convenience, waiting times, frequency of information, and satisfaction with court facilities are associated with satisfaction and happiness to be a witness again. It can be seen from the simplified version of this below (Table 4.3) that there is a proportion of witnesses who appeared not to have specific complaints about, for example, intimidation or the level of information they were given, but were still dissatisfied and would not be willing to be a witness again.

Table 4.3: *Percentage of witnesses saying they were dissatisfied and not happy to be a witness again, by factors associated with satisfaction*

	Dissatisfied and not happy
Not intimidated by individual or process	10
Informed at least once an hour whilst waiting	13
Waited under 4 hours to give evidence	17
Thought verdict was fair	10
Found date convenient	12
Satisfied with the facilities at court	14

Base: All witnesses. Unweighted N=2355.
Note: Excludes 'don't knows'.

Confidence in the CJS

Witnesses were asked how confident they were that the Criminal Justice System:

- Is effective in bringing people who commit crimes to justice

- Meets the needs of victims of crime

- Respects the rights of people accused of committing a crime and treats them fairly

- Deals with cases promptly and efficiently

The same questions are used to measure the CJS objective of improving the level of public confidence in the CJS (Mirrlees-Black, 2001).

Unsurprisingly, victims were least confident about the CJS bringing people to justice (Table 4.4). This was related to their perceptions of the fairness of the verdict: 57 per cent of victims who said they thought the verdict was fair were confident, compared with 25 per cent of victims who said the verdict was unfair. Witnesses at magistrates' courts were more likely than witnesses at the Crown Court to feel confident that the CJS deals with cases promptly and efficiently. As noted in chapter 3, cases at the Crown Court tend to last longer than those at magistrates' courts, so this finding is unsurprising. Table 4.3 also shows that child witnesses were more likely than adults to think that the criminal justice system meets the needs of victims. Perhaps children have fewer preconceptions about how the CJS should deal with victims' needs, and so are less judgemental about the system.

Table 4.4: Confidence in the CJS (percentage saying they were very/fairly confident)

	Bringing people to justice	Meeting the needs of victims	Respecting rights of accused	Dealing with cases promptly and efficiently
Witness type				
Victim	45	52	81	53
Other prosecution	57	59	84	57
Defence	52	57	65	48
Court				
Crown	53	55	80	51
Magistrates'	52	56	81	57
Gender				
Male	54	55	82	55
Female	51	57	79	53
Age				
Under 17	59	66	81	56
17–34	53	62	80	56
35–54	52	50	82	52
55+	46	46	79	52
Total	53	56	81	54

Base: All witnesses. Unweighted N=2496.
Note: Excludes 'don't knows'.

The 2000 British Crime Survey (BCS) asked the same questions to measure confidence in the criminal justice system. The findings showed that levels of confidence were lower for all four measures than those found in the Witness Satisfaction Survey (Mirrlees-Black, 2001).

This might be due to the fact that relatively few victims interviewed in the BCS had an offender brought to justice. Non-reporting to the police is also important as it means that those concerned will not have had contact with the CJS as victims. In addition many of those people interviewed were not victims of crime and therefore had no immediate knowledge of the criminal justice system in practice. In comparison, those surveyed in the Witness Satisfaction Survey had all come to court to give evidence in a case where a defendant was on trial. Both the BCS and the Witness Satisfaction Survey found that, of all four measures of confidence, people were most confident that the system respects the rights of the accused and treats them fairly. However, the majority of witnesses interviewed in the Witness Satisfaction Survey were prosecution witnesses, and it is unsurprising that these witnesses were more likely to feel confident about that aspect of the CJS than defence witnesses. The Witness Satisfaction Survey found that among all witnesses, over half were confident that the criminal justice system met the four measures. The BCS, however, showed that only a quarter were confident that the CJS meets the needs of victims. Table A4.2 gives the comparison between BCS and WSS figures.

Witnesses' confidence in the criminal justice system was also associated with their overall satisfaction, with less confident witnesses feeling less satisfied. Among witnesses who were confident that the CJS meets the needs of victims, 89 per cent said they were satisfied overall, compared with 59 per cent of those who said they were not confident. Table A4.3 shows the relationship between confidence and satisfaction.

Key points

- 76 per cent of witnesses were satisfied with their overall experience

- Satisfaction with each agency was linked with overall satisfaction

- Factors most strongly associated with dissatisfaction are: verdict, intimidation, convenience of date, court facilities and information

- 61 per cent of witnesses were willing to be a witness again

- Willingness increases with age

- Just over a fifth (21%) of witnesses said they were satisfied with their experience but would not want to be a witness again in another trial

- Factors most strongly associated with unwillingness are: intimidation, verdict/ outcome, court facilities, convenience of court date and age

- There are a proportion of witnesses who do not have specific complaints, but who would still not be willing to be a witness again

- Confidence in the CJS varied according to witness type: for example, victims were least confident about the CJS bringing people to justice

- Both the Witness Satisfaction Survey and the British Crime Survey found that people were most confident that the system respects the rights of the accused and treats them fairly

- Confidence in the CJS was associated with overall satisfaction

5.   Conclusion

The Witness Satisfaction Survey 2000 provides the first reliable, national level picture of the extent of witness satisfaction in England and Wales. It showed that 76 per cent of witnesses were satisfied with their overall experience of the criminal justice system. While this may seem fairly high, a figure of nearly one quarter dissatisfied witnesses is not negligible and suggests that there is scope for improvement.

There are some areas related to satisfaction which cannot be addressed, such as verdict. Convenience of court date is also a problematic issue within the current system, in which court listings are arranged to maximise the use of court time and minimise delay. While there is arguably a case for making more effort to arrange court dates which are convenient for witnesses, this would require substantial changes to the listings process and has to be balanced against the need to minimise witness waiting times and more generally against delays to cases which may take some months to reach court.

Excluding verdict and convenience of court date, four key areas relating to witness satisfaction were identified. These were:

- amount of information given to witnesses;

- feelings of intimidation (personal and process);

- facilities at court; and

- waiting times.

These four themes are very closely linked with overall satisfaction. This is not of course an all-inclusive list. There are some factors which are specific to a particular agency or group. One example of this is prosecution witnesses' dissatisfaction with defence lawyers, and defence witnesses' dissatisfaction with prosecution lawyers.

Overall satisfaction was markedly lower than satisfaction with individual agencies. There are a number of reasons which might help to explain this. Firstly, dissatisfaction relating to the four areas mentioned above (information, intimidation, facilities, and waiting times) does not necessarily fall entirely on one agency. For instance, each agency should provide some form of information. Thus, the police should provide information on case progress before court, and court staff information about attending court. Consequently deficiencies in information may not relate to shortcomings of any one agency. Also the experience of intimidation by a person does not necessarily result in dissatisfaction with any one agency; more than one agency may have some responsibility for identifying or taking action to deal with such intimidation. Secondly, witnesses may be broadly satisfied with the performance of each individual agency. However, dissatisfactions which witnesses cannot readily attribute to the performance of a particular agency, or the sum of dissatisfactions across agencies, may be the cause of the relatively lower overall level of satisfaction. Witnesses do not usually have any specialist knowledge of the criminal justice system, and therefore, may not always know who to blame for problems they experience as a witness. Thirdly, there may be an element of dissatisfaction which is not attributable to particular agencies or to aspects of being a witness covered by the survey. The overall experience of being a witness is unlikely to be pleasant for many people, but they may feel they should go through with it in the public interest. They may have been generally treated well by the different agencies within the system, but they still might not have enjoyed the experience.

Despite the generally high levels of satisfaction for individual agencies, satisfaction with each agency varied, and there were areas where each agency could have performed better. Many of these areas directly relate to the four key areas identified above. In addition, satisfaction with all agencies was associated with overall satisfaction – witnesses saying they were fairly or very dissatisfied with, for example, the CPS or defence were more likely to say they were fairly or very dissatisfied with their overall treatment at court. This suggests all agencies could contribute to increased witness satisfaction with the criminal justice system as a whole.

The main findings and implications for each agency are drawn out below. How each individual agency can specifically address the problems with information flow, intimidation (personal and process), facilities (although this is mainly a court issue) and waiting times will be examined.

Police

The police are an important part of witnesses' experience of the criminal justice system: in most cases they will be the first point of contact a witness has with the system.

Satisfaction with the police was relatively high, at 88 per cent, and was associated with courteous treatment and how regularly or whether witnesses were kept informed. Almost half (44%) of victim witnesses said they were not kept informed at all by the police. This seems a high proportion, especially in light of the standard set for the police in the Victim's Charter, which states that they should keep victims informed of significant developments in the case. Almost all (98%) of witnesses who said they were kept regularly informed by the police were satisfied with the treatment they received from the police.

Intimidation is also an area in which the role of the police is crucial. Their role is mainly relevant in relation to pre-court intimidation, but as was mentioned in chapter 3, 35 per cent of witnesses who felt intimidated said they felt intimidated before coming to court. The police can only do something about intimidation if it is reported or if they detect it without a report. There are indications that the police are becoming increasingly attuned to the possibility of intimidation. Thus, ACPO advice to assist in the identification of intimidated witnesses will be published shortly. The issue of process intimidation can only really be covered inasmuch as police need to be supportive and helpful towards witnesses whilst they are at court. The survey showed that witnesses who were treated courteously by the police were less likely to feel intimidated both by the process and by a person.

Victim Support

About a third of victim witnesses had contact with Victim Support. Victims of a violent or sexual offence were more likely to have contact. The same pattern was reported in the British Crime Survey. The Witness Satisfaction Survey found that the majority (88%) of those who had contact with Victim Support were very or fairly satisfied with the way they were treated.

Victims were asked whether they were provided with details of follow-up support for after the court case, and if not, whether they would have liked such support. Among victim witnesses who did not receive follow-up support, half would have liked to. This is a high demand, which could be addressed by Victim Support. However, there may be resource issues to consider.

Victim Support may also have a role in being particularly alert to the possibility of witness intimidation, as well as helping witnesses in reducing fears about process intimidation. The service is of course confidential, but sometimes intimidated witnesses may wish to discuss with Victim Support how they should deal with their fears, and this may include discussing whether they wish to tell the police, or to have help in so doing.

Court staff

Satisfaction with court staff was high (96%) among all witnesses.[27] Most witnesses also said they felt they were treated courteously by court staff. This is a reassuring finding as court staff on reception are usually the first point of contact for witnesses arriving at the Crown Court or magistrates' courts. More can be done by court staff, however, to make the experience for witnesses better. Not all witnesses who reported to reception on arrival were shown where to go, and for those who did not report to reception it was not always clear where they needed to go.

Some witnesses were dissatisfied with the facilities at court, and some of the areas of dissatisfaction could be addressed by court authorities. These include the state of the toilets and refreshment facilities. Some witnesses stated that they could not find or were not shown where the canteen was. In some cases there were no refreshment facilities at all. Some witnesses also mentioned that they did not feel there were enough amenities to occupy their time. Suggestions included providing more reading materials or television access.

Court staff could provide witnesses with information prior to coming to court about likely waiting times, and also advise them to bring reading material to court.

Court staff also have a potential role in relation to both personal and process intimidation. They can help to put witnesses at ease and also help in ensuring separate waiting facilities wherever possible. Where this is not a feasible option, there are other means of keeping witnesses apart: for instance, the use of pagers or mobile phones to inform witnesses when they are to be called. This would mean that witnesses could wait outside the court environment. Also, court staff have a role in making screens available in the courtroom for vulnerable and intimidated witnesses to help minimise feelings of intimidation by defendants.

Witness Service

Providing witnesses with information, support and explaining basic court procedures are just some of the ways in which the Witness Service (WS) can help witnesses to feel more at ease.

---

27 This can be compared with the LCD Juror Satisfaction Survey 2000 which shows that satisfaction among jurors with their treatment by the court generally (and not just court staff) is also high, at 95 per cent. *The User Satisfaction Survey 2001: Wave 1*, which was carried out on behalf of the Court Service, is also relevant. This looked at members of the public who had used the civil courts, professionals at both the civil and criminal courts, and jurors. 79 per cent of users who responded to the survey were satisfied with the overall service provided by the courts (again, this is not just limited to court staff).

Satisfaction with the WS was high (97% who had contact said they were very or fairly satisfied). However, only half of all witnesses had contact. Over a third (37%) of witnesses who did not have contact would have liked some support. This suggests the extension of the WS to all criminal courts by April 2002 will increase overall witness satisfaction. The second sweep of the survey should show a greater and clearer effect of this than would be possible if we took another snapshot now (the Witness Service has been expanding since the first survey was conducted). However, even in those courts that currently have a WS it appears that some witnesses are unaware of its existence, or what it does. Contact with a witness co-ordinator in advance of the case is of obvious benefit to witnesses.

Although the majority of witnesses felt that the Witness Service was able to explain everything they did not understand about the court process, in a minority of cases (about 6%) they felt they could not. Offering support to more witnesses, or explaining in more detail what is available to them, in terms of both familiarisation visits, or the opportunity to look round a court room on the day could go a long way in helping some witnesses who do not know of these procedures. Other agencies, especially the police, lawyers and court staff could help ensure that people are aware of the support available. In relation to waiting times, the WS could offer advice and reassurance to witnesses.

The role of the Witness Service in relation to witnesses' fears about personal and process intimidation is also crucial. Being available to wait with the witness outside the courtroom and then to accompany them into court might help in relieving some intimidation before going into court. Also, by sharing information with other agencies, measures against intimidation could be taken.

Lawyers

Satisfaction was higher for CPS lawyers than defence lawyers, but this probably reflects the fact that the great majority of witnesses interviewed were prosecution witnesses – who tended to be less satisfied with defence lawyers than all other groups. Most prosecution witnesses (89%) were satisfied with the CPS, and 92 per cent of defence witnesses were satisfied with defence lawyers.

Just under half of witnesses (45%) had contact with the lawyer working on 'their side' outside the courtroom. These witnesses were asked whether the lawyer explained who they were and whether they were able to answer any questions they might have had. Not all witnesses said that the lawyer explained who they were or felt that the lawyer was able to answer their questions. This is an area of possible improvement. The Victim's Charter

Standard says that it is the responsibility of a representative of the CPS to introduce themselves whilst the victim is waiting and tell them what to expect. Only 48 per cent of victim witnesses had contact with the lawyer other than being questioned in court. It is possible that lawyers may also have a role in relation to reducing dissatisfaction with waiting times at court. They are particularly well placed to explain to witnesses the reasons for any delays in calling them.

Whether witnesses felt they were treated courteously and whether they felt they were given the opportunity to say everything they wanted to when being questioned in court were strongly associated with how satisfied they subsequently felt. Witnesses could perhaps be informed in advance about the general nature of questioning that they might expect from lawyers in the courtroom (although it is vital that any accusation that witnesses were 'coached' should be avoided). Witnesses might be told, for example, that they will be expected to answer questions and may not be able to give as full an account of what happened as they would wish. If witnesses' expectations were addressed – and in some cases challenged – at an earlier stage, they might enter court in a realistic frame of mind and be less disappointed if they found that they were not able to say all they wanted when giving evidence. When questioning witnesses, lawyers should stay within the boundaries of professional codes of conduct. Also, treating witnesses courteously and reasonably is in the public interest, because any reports of ill-treatment of witnesses that become public knowledge may discourage others from testifying in the future.

Although facilities at court are not the responsibility of lawyers, they ought as a minimum to satisfy themselves that their witnesses are comfortable.

Judges and magistrates

Satisfaction with treatment by judges and magistrates was high: 95 per cent of witnesses felt very or fairly satisfied, with only 5 per cent fairly or very dissatisfied. The 1998 BCS (Mattinson and Mirrlees-Black, 2000) found that 17 per cent of respondents thought that magistrates did a poor or very poor job. This figure was higher, at 26 per cent, for judges. However, witnesses in the Witness Survey were not asked whether they thought judges and magistrates did a *good* job, and it is difficult to know how they would have responded. It might be important, however, to note that witnesses have first hand knowledge of and contact with magistrates and judges, whereas most of the general public (i.e. many interviewed in the BCS) would not have had such contact. The BCS questioned respondents who had not necessarily had any contact with judges or magistrates.

One possible reason for the high level of satisfaction with judges and magistrates might be a lack of understanding of their role. Witnesses might actually have quite low expectations, not realising judges and magistrates can, for example, intervene to stop lawyers asking double-barrelled questions. Half of witnesses said that the judge or magistrate said something to them whilst they were giving evidence. This had no effect on how satisfied with their treatment from judges or magistrates the witnesses subsequently felt. The survey did not ask, however, whether the judge or magistrate intervened when the lawyer asked the witness questions. Most witnesses (97%) felt that they were treated courteously by the judge or magistrate in their case. For those who did not, however, satisfaction with judges and magistrates was lower.

Judges and magistrates can help reduce process intimidation by explaining procedures to witnesses and by putting them at ease as much as possible. Treating witnesses courteously should also help reduce this type of intimidation. It is also very much magistrates' and judges' responsibility to be alive to the possibility of personal intimidation, for example, from the defendant and the public gallery. In cases where it is appropriate, the use of screens in court might help alleviate some of witnesses' anxieties.

Concluding comments

It can be seen that all agencies have a role to play in helping to increase witness satisfaction, both with the individual agency involved, but also overall. The chapter will finish with addressing each of the four areas that have been identified as intimately linked with satisfaction and suggest ways forward for improving agencies' performance.

Information

Keeping witnesses informed at all stages of the process of being a witness is vital if satisfaction is to increase. Each agency within the CJS has responsibility for this, and appropriate information must be made available by each individual agency and at every stage. This means keeping witnesses informed before they arrive at court, and during the day while they are waiting to give evidence. Another area that needs to be addressed is that of notifying witnesses as early as possible about the date of the court case as this might help reduce the numbers of those who found the date very inconvenient. Although there is probably little that can be done to change witnesses' views of whether a fair verdict was reached, some witnesses do not even get to hear the outcome of the case in which they gave evidence and this is a cause of discontent. It would be relatively straightforward to inform all witnesses of the outcome of the case in which they appeared. The issue of who should be responsible for this task would of course have to be resolved.

Intimidation

Tackling the causes of both personal and process intimidation would go a long way towards securing more satisfied witnesses. Each agency can be involved to some degree in helping identify witness intimidation (of both kinds) and in reassuring witnesses and providing the support they require. The police and Victim Support should be alive to the possibility of personal witness intimidation before the witness gets to court. At court, the Witness Service can do much to alleviate fears of the process of giving evidence. Lawyers can introduce themselves and talk to the witnesses about what to expect in the courtroom, especially if the witness has not been able to have a pre-court familiarisation visit. In the courtroom, judges and magistrates can explain procedures to witnesses, treat them courteously, and stop unnecessary questioning by lawyers. Lawyers should respect witnesses and follow professional codes of conduct when questioning them. In cases which involve vulnerable and intimidated witnesses, all possible assistance should be provided to reduce further intimidation. The scope for doing so will increase when the special measures for vulnerable and intimidated witnesses provided for in the Youth Justice and Criminal Evidence Act 1999 come into effect.

Waiting times

Witnesses should be informed about the time they may be expected to wait to give evidence and be given updates about what is happening during their wait. This is particularly relevant in the minority of cases where the wait is likely to be more than four hours. It is frustrating for witnesses to be kept waiting, but it is even more of an issue when they do not know why. Stress levels are likely to increase if the witness is hanging around and does not know when they are likely to be called. When the court knows that there is going to be a delay, witnesses could be given the opportunity of leaving the court building and being called back nearer the time of being needed to give their evidence. This would mean that they were not left waiting near the defendant or other people who might intimidate them. Witnesses who were given no information while they were waiting and who had to wait for longer than four hours to be called were even less satisfied. This suggests that reducing waiting times would have most effect if it was combined with a target to improve the amount of information given.

Court facilities

Letting witnesses know what facilities are available to them at court before they arrive, and then showing them where these facilities are on arrival, is an important and perhaps under-estimated component of witnesses' sense of well-being at court. This could be through a familiarisation visit or a leaflet sent at the time of inviting the witness to court. As far as possible, prosecution and defence witnesses should be given separate waiting areas and toilets. This would also help to reduce intimidation.

Conclusion

The above programme of action on the part of the different criminal justice agencies would go a long way towards addressing the concerns which witnesses expressed during the survey and perhaps help to raise overall satisfaction beyond the fairly high level at which it is currently pitched. While the experience of giving evidence can probably never be made pleasant, a range of relatively straightforward amendments to the way in which witnesses are dealt with may go a long way towards removing some of the factors which irritate or even frighten those who fulfil this vital role.

Table A2.1: *Percentage of witnesses saying they were very/fairly satisfied with their treatment by the police*

	Satisfied with police
Witness type	
Victim	86
Other prosecution	91
Defence	78
Court type	
Crown	87
Magistrate	89
Sex	
Male	90
Female	86
Age	
Under 17	94
17–34	86
35–54	89
55+	92
Ethnicity	
White	88
Black	92
Asian	90
Other	86
Total	88

Base: All who had contact with the police. Unweighted N=2122.
Note: Excludes 'don't knows'.

Table A2.2: **Percentage of witnesses who said they were concerned about being a witness, by offence type**

	Violence/sexual	Other	Total
Male	52	41	46
Female	71	64	68
Total – all witnesses	61	50	56

Base: All witnesses. Unweighted N=2498.

Table A2.3: **Percentage of witnesses saying they were given enough information, by witness type**

	Victim	Other prosecution	Defence
Time involved in being a witness	29	31	22
What needed to bring	26	31	17
Time needed to arrive	89	90	81
Directions to court	63	63	46
What to do on arrival	52	55	32
What would happen in court	50	56	40

Base: All witnesses. Unweighted N=2498.
Note: Excludes 'don't knows'.

Table A3.1: Percentage showing when witnesses received support from the Witness Service

	In courtroom	After giving evidence
Witness type		
Victim	28	45
Prosecution	23	38
Defence	27	33
Court type		
Crown	29	47
Magistrate	17	27
Sex		
Male	18	31
Female	32	49
Age		
Under 17	21	45
17–34	24	42
35–54	27	37
55+	21	37
Total	25	40

Base: All respondents who had contact with the Witness Service. Unweighted N=1273.
Note: Respondents could have had support from the Witness Service both in the
   courtroom and after giving evidence.

Table A3.2: **Whether witnesses had the opportunity to look round a court room before the case began (percentages)**

	Yes – given opportunity	Already had visit before the day	No – not given opportunity
Witness type			
Prosecution	46	3	51
Defence	26	2	72
Court type			
Crown	51	5	44
Magistrate	37	2	61
Sex			
Male	43	2	56
Female	45	5	51
Age			
Under 17	53	11	36
17+	43	2	55
Total	44	3	53

Base: All witnesses. Unweighted N=2483.
Note: Excludes 'don't knows'.

Table A3.3: Treatment of witnesses in the court room by the other side's lawyer (percentages)

	Treated courteously by other side's lawyer	Given opportunity to say everything
Witness type		
Victim	45	40
Other prosecution	67	69
Defence	64	67
Court type		
Crown	64	61
Magistrate	57	60
Sex		
Male	64	65
Female	55	55
Age		
Under 17	38	52
17–34	54	58
35–54	66	60
55+	83	79
Total	60	61

Base: Unweighted N=1280.
Note: Excludes 'don't knows'.

Table A4.1: Percentage of witnesses saying they were very/fairly satisfied with each agency within the CJS, by witness type

	Police	CPS/ prosecution lawyer	Defence lawyer	Court staff	Victim Support	Witness Service	Judge/ Magistrate	Overall
Victim	86	82	45	95	88	97	92	67
Other prosecution	91	92	69	97	-	97	97	80
Defence	78	68	92	95	-	94	95	77

Base: All witnesses. Unweighted N=2498.
Note: Excludes 'don't knows'.

Table A4.2: Confidence in the CJS – comparison with BCS and WSS data (percentage saying they were very or fairly confident)

	Bringing people to justice	Meeting the needs of victims	Respecting rights of accused	Dealing with cases promptly and efficiently
British Crime Survey	46	26	69	34
Witness Satisfaction Survey	53	56	81	54

Note: Excludes 'don't knows'.

Table A4.3: Overall satisfaction by confidence in the CJS (percentages)

	Overall satisfaction
Bringing people to justice	
Confident	88
Not confident	62
Meeting the needs of victims	
Confident	89
Not confident	59
Respecting the rights of people accused	
Confident	80
Not confident	63
Dealing with cases promptly and efficiently	
Confident	87
Not confident	63
Total	76

Base: All witnesses. Unweighted N=2498.
Note: Excludes 'don't knows'.

Table A4.4: Logistic regression model predicting overall dissatisfaction among all witnesses

Factor	Dissatisfaction Exp. (B)
Verdict	
Thought verdict fair	1.00
Thought verdict unfair	4.53
No opinion	1.94
Did not know verdict	2.22
Whether intimidated	
No	1.00
Yes - by individual only	1.93
Yes - by process only	2.84
Yes - by both	5.03
Convenience of date	
Convenient	1.00
Slightly inconvenient	1.49
Very inconvenient	2.70
Satisfaction with facilities	
Satisfied	1.00
Not satisfied	2.60
Info on what would happen at court	
Enough	1.00
None	1.88
Frequency of information	
At least once an hour	1.00
Given no info	2.06
Whether victim	
Non-victim	1.00
Victim	1.76

Base: All witnesses. Unweighted N=2283.

Notes: 1. All differences are statistically significant. A 'B' coefficient greater than 1 indicates a relative risk of dissatisfaction greater than the reference group.
2. Overall prediction rate 81% accurate (94% satisfied, 40% dissatisfied).

Table A4.5: Logistic regression model predicting overall dissatisfaction among witnesses who gave evidence in court

Factor	Dissatisfaction Exp. (B)
Verdict	
Thought verdict fair	1.00
Thought verdict unfair	4.23
No opinion	2.85
Did not know verdict	1.73
Whether intimidated	
No	1.00
Yes - by individual only	1.53
Yes - by process only	2.43
Yes - by both	6.54
Convenience of date	
Convenient	1.00
Slightly inconvenient	1.58
Very inconvenient	2.83
Satisfaction with facilities	
Satisfied	1.00
Not satisfied	2.75
Courteous treatment by own lawyer	
Yes	1.00
No	2.44
Given opportunity to say everything by own lawyer	
Yes	1.00
No	3.45
Whether victim	
Non-victim	1.00
Victim	2.46
Waiting to give evidence	
Under 4 hours	1.00
Over 4 hours	2.15

Base: Witnesses who gave evidence. Unweighted N=1389.
Notes: 1. Includes witnesses who gave evidence in court.
        2. All differences are statistically significant. A 'B' coefficient greater than 1 indicates a relative risk of dissatisfaction greater than the reference group.
        3. Overall prediction rate 82% accurate (94% satisfied, 44% dissatisfied).

Table A4.6: *Logistic regression model predicting overall dissatisfaction among witnesses who did not give evidence in court*

Factor	Dissatisfaction Exp. (B)
Verdict	
Thought verdict fair	1.00
Thought verdict unfair	3.49
Did not know verdict	3.78
Whether intimidated	
No	1.00
Yes - by individual only	2.22
Yes - by process only	2.61
Yes - by both	2.58
Convenience of date	
Convenient	1.00
Slightly inconvenient	1.54
Very inconvenient	3.24
Satisfaction with facilities	
Satisfied	1.00
Not satisfied	2.91
Info on time involved in being a witness	
Enough	1.00
None	2.40
Frequency of information	
At least once an hour	1.00
Given no info	3.16

Base: Witnesses who did not give evidence. Unweighted N=899.

Notes: 1. All differences are statistically significant. A 'B' coefficient greater than 1 indicates a relative risk of dissatisfaction greater than the reference group.

2. Overall prediction rate 82% accurate (96% satisfied, 35% dissatisfied).

Table A4.7: Logistic regression model predicting unwillingness among witnesses to be a witness again

Factor	Unwillingness Exp. (B)
Verdict	
Thought verdict fair	1.00
Thought verdict unfair	2.27
Whether intimidated	
No	1.00
Yes - by individual only	1.75
Yes - by process only	2.42
Yes - by both	3.91
Convenience of date	
Convenient	1.00
Slightly inconvenient	1.60
Very inconvenient	2.75
Satisfaction with facilities	
Satisfied	1.00
Not satisfied	2.08
Information on how much time would be involved	
Enough	1.00
None	1.96
Witness type	
Prosecution	1.00
Victim	1.47
Defence	1.49
Age group	
Adult (17+)	1.00
Child (under 17)	2.22
Sex	
Male	1.00
Female	1.59

Base: All witnesses. Unweighted N=2268.

Note: All differences are statistically significant. A 'B' coefficient greater than 1 indicates a relative risk of unwillingness greater than the reference group.
Overall prediction rate 71% accurate (84% willing, 50% unwilling).

Table A4.8: Overall satisfaction and happiness to be a witness again, by various factors associated with satisfaction (percentages)

	Satisfied and happy	Satisfied but not happy	Dissatisfied but happy	Dissatisfied and not happy
Intimidation				
Individual only	45	25	6	24
Process only	37	23	8	32
Both ind. and process	18	21	8	53
Neither	65	20	6	10
Information				
At least once an hour	59	22	5	13
Less than once an hour	54	17	6	22
Not waiting long enough	63	20	7	10
No information	40	22	9	29
Waiting to give evidence				
Under 4 hours	56	22	6	17
Over 4 hours	40	25	8	27
Did not give evidence	57	20	6	17
Whether thought verdict fair				
Yes	64	22	4	10
No	35	21	11	32
No opinion	60	16	8	17
Don't know	56	18	6	20
Whether date was convenient				
Convenient	63	19	6	12
Slightly inconvenient	51	25	7	18
Very inconvenient	33	24	8	35
Whether satisfied with facilities				
Yes	59	21	6	14
No	34	22	8	37
Total	55	21	6	18

Note: Excludes 'don't knows'.

Home Office (1996) *The Victim's Charter.* London: Home Office.

Home Office (1998) *Speaking Up For Justice: Report of the Interdepartmental Working Group on the treatment of Vulnerable and Intimidated Witnesses in the Criminal Justice System.* London: Home Office.

Home Office (1999) *Criminal Justice System Strategic Plan 1999–2002.* London: Home Office.

Levesley, T. (2001) *User Satisfaction Survey 2001.* Unpublished report for the Lord Chancellor's Department.

Lord Chancellor's Department (1998) *Joint Performance Management Witness Monitoring Survey.* Unpublished report.

Lord Chancellor's Department (2000) *Juror Satisfaction Survey 2000.* Unpublished report.

Lord Chancellor's Department (2001) *Magistrates' Courts Annual Report on National Performance Indicators (NPI's) 2000/2001.* Compiled by Business Performance Branch, Magistrates' Courts Division. London: Lord Chancellor's Department.

Lees, S. (1996) *Carnal Knowledge: Rape on Trial.* London: Penguin.

Maguire, M. and Kynch, J. (2000) *Victim Support: Findings from the 1998 British Crime Survey* Home Office Research, Development and Statistics Directorate Research Findings 117. London: Home Office.

Mattinson, J. and Mirrlees-Black, C. (2000) *Attitudes to Crime and Criminal Justice: Findings from the 1998 British Crime Survey.* Home Office Research, Development and Statistics Directorate Home Office Research Study 200. London: Home Office.

Maynard, W. (1994) *Witness Intimidation: Strategies for Prevention.* Police Research Group Crime Detection and Prevention Series Paper 55. London: Home Office.

Mews, A. and Peacock, J. (2001) *Magistrates' Courts Waiting Times on the Day and User Reaction Surveys, 2000*. Information Bulletin Issue 1. London: Lord Chancellor's Department.

Mirrlees-Black, C. (2001) *Confidence in the Criminal Justice System: Findings from the 2000 British Crime Survey.* Home Office Research, Development and Statistics Directorate Research Findings 137. London: Home Office.

Plotnikoff, J. and Woolfson, R. (1997) *Options for improved support for victims and other witnesses attending magistrates' courts: report for the Home Office.* Unpublished report.

Plotnikoff, J. and Woolfson, R. (1998) *Witness Care in Magistrates' Courts and The Youth Court.* Home Office Research and Statistics Directorate Research Findings 68. London: Home Office.

Southgate, P. and Grosvenor, T. (2000), *'Confidence in the Criminal Justice System – A Qualitative Study' in Promoting Confidence in the Criminal Justice System.* Report to a Workshop held 10th February 2000.

Sims, L. and Myhill, A. *Policing and the Public: Findings from the 2000 British Crime Survey.* Home Office Research, Development and Statistics Directorate Research Findings 136. London: Home Office.

Tarling, R., Dowds, L. and Budd, T. (2000) *Victim and Witness Intimidation: Key Findings from the British Crime Survey.* Home Office Research, Development and Statistics Directorate Research Findings 124. London: Home Office.

Notes

RDS Publications

Requests for Publications

Copies of our publications and a list of those currently available may be obtained from:

Home Office
Research, Development and Statistics Directorate
Communications & Development Unit
Room 275, Home Office
50 Queen Anne's Gate
London SW1H 9AT
Telephone: 020 7273 2084 (answerphone outside of office hours)
Facsimile: 020 7222 0211
E-mail: publications.rds@homeoffice.gsi.gov.uk

alternatively

why not visit the RDS web-site at
          Internet: http://www.homeoffice.gov.uk/rds/index.htm

where many of our publications are available to be read on screen or downloaded for printing.